P9-DTE-424

INSTRUCTOR'S MANUAL

ECONOMETRIC ANALYSIS

An Applications Approach

James L. Doti
Chapman College

Esmael Adibi
Chapman College

Prentice Hall, Englewood Cliffs, New Jersey 07632

© 1988 by **PRENTICE-HALL, INC.**
A Division of Simon & Schuster
Englewood Cliffs, N.J. 07632

ISBN: 0-13-224122-6

Printed in the United States of America

Table of Contents

Chapter 6 – Using Other Econometric Techniques

A Note to Instructors

Our book, *Econometric Analysis*, is designed for an introductory level course in econometrics that emphasizes computer applications. A data disk accompanies the book and *Computer Sessions* and *Computer Exercises* that utilize the popular MicroTSP econometrics software are integrated throughout the text to reinforce the development of econometric tools of analysis. Since all computer usage in the text is self-directed, the instructor can emphasize the development and interpretation of econometric theory in class lectures rather than get bogged down with constructing a data bank or teaching computer techniques.

Our class format is to collect homework at the beginning of the class, answer student questions, and review the prior week's homework. The remainder of class time is spent discussing the development of econometric tools and their application in econometric analysis.

Our students are expected to replicate all the *Computer Sessions* within each section on their own. Completing these sessions should give students the requisite skills to complete the *Computer Exercises* at the end of each section. We generally assign two to three *Questions for Review* and one to two *Computer Exercises* per student. We have also found it useful to assign one *Study Project* to each student or team of students at the beginning of the semester and have them turn in a written report or make an oral presentation in class regarding the assigned project.

The computer-related exercises require about two hours of "hands-on" personal computer usage per week for each student. For econometric classes at Chapman College, we have found it helpful to establish a computer reservation schedule the first week of class. If students do not purchase individual packages of the student version of MicroTSP, students can use MicroTSP diskettes that are placed in the computer lab and made available to students on a check-out basis. As for additional expenses, each student need only purchase two blank diskettes.

Although the concept of the derivative in calculus is presented in a few isolated examples in the text, an understanding of the basic material in the text can be obtained with only a rudimentary knowledge of algebra. In terms of the required background in statistics, a prior course in elementary statistics will allow students the opportunity to spend more time on the econometric applications and less time on learning the derivation of the various statistical tools described in the text.

If this book is used as a supplementary text, it might be useful to refer to the comparison of *Computer Sessions* and *Computer Exercises* with the relevant chapters in several econometrics texts as shown on pages v - vi of this *Manual*.

A suggested outline for a fifteen week course is as follows:

Week:	Section:	Week:	Section:	Week:	Section:
1	1.1–2.1	6	4.1–4.2	11	5.3
2	2.2	7	4.3–4.4	12	6.1
3	3.1	8	4.5	13	6.2
4	3.2	9	5.1	14	6.3
5	3.3	10	5.2	15	Review

For longer sessions, the topics can be covered in more depth; for shorter sessions, Section 3.1 on computer graphing and Section 6.3 on simultaneous equations can be omitted. Because of the building-block approach used in the book, the subject matter is best covered in sequential order.

We welcome any comments for improving the book or this *Manual* and can be reached at the following address:

Albers School of Business
Seattle University
Seattle, Washington 98122

Arrangement of Compter Sessions and Exercises to Conform with Other Textbooks

After studying the *Computer Sessions* and completing the *Computer Exercises* in Section 2.2, 3.1 and 3.2 (optional), subsequent sessions and exercises can be arranged to conform to the subject order of the following textbooks:

Computer Session:	Computer Exercises:	Econometric Models and Economic Forecasts, 2nd Ed. R. Pindyck & D. Rubinfeld	Introduction to Econometrics, 2nd Ed. H. Kelejian & W. Oates	Econometrics, 2nd Ed. R. Wonnacott & T. Wonnacott
3.3-1	3.3-9	None	None	None
3.3-2	3.3-10	2.2	2.1	5-1
	3.3-11			
4.2-1	4.2-5	3.1	2.4	2-4
	4.2-6			
	4.2-7			
4.2-2	4.2-8	3.1	3.4	2-4
4.4-1	4.4-6	3.3	3.1	2-8
	4.4-7			
4.5-1	4.5-4	4.2	4.2	3-1
	4.5-5			
4.5-2	4.5-6	8.1	3.5	6-6
	4.5-7			
4.5-3	4.5-8	8.1	3.5	6-6
4.5-4	4.5-9	8.1	4.5	3-2
5.1-1	5.1-8	4.4	4.2	3-4
5.1-2	5.1-9	4.4	6.1	3-4
5.1-3	5.1-10	4.4	6.1	3-6
5.1-4	5.1-11	4.4	6.1	3-6
5.2-1	5.2-7	6.2	6.2	6-7
	5.2-9			
	5.2-10			
5.2-2	5.2-8	8.2	6.2	6-7
5.2-3	5.2-11	6.2	6.2	6-7
5.2-4	5.2-12	6.2	6.2	6-7
5.3-1	5.3-6	6.1	6.3	6-1
5.3-2	5.3-7	6.1	6.3	6-1
5.3-3	5.3-8	6.1	6.3	6-1
5.3-4	5.3-9	6.1	6.3	6-1

Computer Session:	Computer Exercises:	Econometric Models and Economic Forecasts, 2nd Ed. R. Pindyck & D. Rubinfeld	Introduction to Econometrics, 2nd Ed. H. Kelejian & W. Oates	Econometrics, 2nd Ed. R. Wonnacott & T. Wonnacott
6.1-1	None	Shown in Examples	3.2	4-3
6.1-2	6.1-6 6.1-8	" "	3.2	4-4
6.1-3	6.1-7	" "	3.2	4-4
6.1-4	6.1-7	" "	5.3	4-4
6.1-5	None	" "	5.3	4-4
6.2-1	6.2-8 6.2-9 6.2-11	9.1	3.4	6-8
6.2-2	6.2-7	5.2	5.2	4-1
6.2-3	6.2-10	5.2	5.2	6-4
6.2-4	None	9.1	5.1	6-8
6.2-5	None	9.1	5.1	6-8
6.3-1	6.3-8 6.3-11	7.3	7.2	9.3
6.3-2	6.3-9	7.6	7.5	9-1
6.3-3	6.3-11	7.7	7.6	9-1
6.3-4	None	7.6	7.6	9-1

2.1 Exercises

Questions for Review:

2.1-1.   This qualitative statement can be interpreted quantitatively by using data such as: (1) The amount of snow dropped during some time period; (2) A given number of automobiles left stranded; or (3) A given percentage of public transit vehicles (i.e., buses, commuter trains) not able to operate.

2.1-2.   a. Cross-section   d. Neither - qualitative data
         b. Cross-section   e. Time-series
         c. Cross-section   f. Both time-series and cross section

2.1-3.

Name	Classification	Name	Classification
GEX	Flow	MNS	Stock
GPS	Flow	PRR	Stock
GSL	Flow	AAA	Stock
TFG	Flow	MTR	Stock
TSL	Flow	UNP	Stock
PDE	Stock	NUS	Stock

2.1-4.   *Note to instructor:*   The point of this question is to familiarize the student with the contents of Tables 2.1-1 and 2.1-2.

a. *Historical Statistics of the U.S.; Survey of Current Business;* and *Federal Reserve Bulletin*
b. *Fortune 500 Directory* and *Moody's Manuals*
c. *State and Metropolitan Area Data Book*
d. *World Statistics in Brief*
e. *Advertising Age Yearbook*
f. *Census of Population and Housing* and *Editor and Publisher Marketing Guide*

2.1-5.   Arbitrarily select December, 1970 as the overlapping period:

$$\text{Transform } 119.1 \text{ to } 138.5$$
$$119.1(x) = 138.5$$
$$x = 138.5/119.1 = \underline{1.162883}$$

$$\text{Jan., 1971} \quad 119.2 * 1.162883 = \underline{138.6}$$
$$\text{Feb., 1971} \quad 119.4 * 1.162883 = \underline{138.8}$$

2.1-6   Arbitrarily select January, 1970 as the overlapping period:

$$\text{Transform } 149.6 \text{ to } 117.1$$
$$149.6(x) = 117.1$$
$$x = 117.1/149.6 = \underline{0.78275401}$$

1

$$\text{Feb., 1971} \qquad 150.7 * 0.78275401 = \underline{118.0}$$

Study Projects:

2.1-7.   *Note to instructor:* A library visitation of the class to the reference section during the first week of class may be a useful way to approach this topic.   During such a visitation, library resources relating to those discussed in Study Projects 2.1-9 and 2.1-11 can also be covered.

2.1-8.   *Note to instructor:* If a sample area other than Chicago or Orange County is selected for analysis in subsequent computer exercises, it would be extremely useful to obtain quarterly data on construction valuation for the sample area.   These data should cover the same geographic area defined for local employment and be similar in definition to that of BTO and BTO1.

2.1-9.   See Exercise 2.1-7.

2.1-10.   *Note to instructor:* It may be useful to point out to the student that finding the appropriate data is like doing "detective work." For example, if the student starts with *Historical Statistics of the U.S.* to find the quarterly price deflator series (PDE), only annual data will be found. But before each data section in *Historical Statistics*, sources are given for more detailed statistics.   In the case of the price deflator, the source given for quarterly data (1972=100) is *National Income and Product Accounts of the U.S. 1929-1976* (Table 7.1 pp. 320-321).

	PDE		PDE		PDE		PDE
1955:1	60.27	1958:1	65.63	1961:1	68.88	1964:1	72.36
2	60.65	2	65.79	2	69.22	2	72.57
3	61.03	3	66.17	3	69.54	3	72.97
4	61.40	4	66.47	4	69.65	4	73.16
1956:1	61.91	1959:1	67.04	1962:1	70.23	1965:1	73.77
2	62.43	2	67.55	2	70.48	2	74.13
3	63.13	3	67.81	3	70.62	3	74.56
4	63.69	4	68.00	4	71.08	4	74.96
1957:1	64.40	1960:1	68.44	1963:1	71.41		
2	64.65	2	68.56	2	71.46		
3	65.28	3	68.86	3	71.66		
4	65.37	4	68.96	4	72.17		

2.1-11   *Note to instructor:* Most BLS offices report on a monthly basis and revise to a benchmark figure once a year.   The actual timing, however, differs for the various offices.

2

2.2 Exercises

Questions for Review:

2.2-1.   Numerical data bases contain actual quantitative data while bibliographic data contain information that makes it possible to find specific data series, sources, references and citations.

2.2-2.   Numerical data bases are continually updated and revised. When presented in seasonally adjusted form or in real terms, data bases have the additional benefit of being measured using a consistent seasonal adjustment technique and common base year. The software that usually accompanies numerical data bases also makes redefining, transforming and conducting statistical tests on the data a relatively simple task.

2.2-3.   The active memory of the computer is like a desk top in that it contains information currently being used, while the non-active memory is like a desk drawer in that it includes information stored on data disks. For example, as data are entered in the computer using the data editor of MicroTSP, the data become part of the active memory of the computer. When these data are entered on a disk using the *STORE* command, a copy of the relevant data in the active memory will become part of the non-active memory of the computer. When the computer is turned off, all the data in the active memory are "lost," and only that which has been stored in the non-active memory can be retrieved for use at a later time in the active memory of the computer.

2.2-4.   The *R* and *C* commands rename and catalog the files in the active memory of the computer while the *REN* and *CAT* commands rename and catalog the files on the disk (i.e., non-active memory of the computer).

2.2-5.   The following command can be entered to delete the double entry: >*X67.3*.

2.2-6.   Avoid using those observations in a time series that may be subject to significant revisions. The observations in a series likely to be subject to such revisions are usually the most currently published. Data that exhibit erratic historical patterns are also likely to experience sharper revisions than more stable series. For these reasons, it is recommended that the most current unrevised "preliminary" estimates in highly erratic series be excluded from statistical tests.

2.2-7.   Whenever the accuracy of a series is in doubt, it should clearly be stated in the reported research results. If possible, the empirical analysis should be repeated using alternative data.

3

Computer Exercises:

2.2-8.   Follow procedures in Computer Session 2.2-2 after formatting a disk to be used as a work files disk:

A>*FORMAT B:*

2.2-9.   Follow procedures in Computer Session 2.2-2 for copying a disk.   Copy the original data disk for use as a backup:

A>*DISKCOPY A: B:*

2.2-10.   Follow procedures in Computer Session 2.2-3.

Study Projects:

2.2-11.   See Exercise 2.1-7 in the previous section.

2.2-12.   A description of these procedures can be obtained from the local BLS office.

2.2-13.   Extra-credit assignment for student or team of students.

2.2-14.   Extra-credit assignment for student or team of students.

3.1   Exercises

Questions for Review:

3.1-1.   The *SMPL* command is used to set the sample period over which the various MicroTSP operations are performed.   Notice, however, that the current sample period specified by the *SMPL* command does not affect the period over which the *FETCH* command operates.   An entire file is fetched no matter what sample period is set.   All other commands, including the *STORE* command, are performed over the sample period in effect at the time the command is executed.

3.1-2.   One possible error would occur if quarterly data are available only from 1965:1 to 1983:4 and the following commands are entered:

>*SMPL 65.1 83.4*
>*GENR PGNP=((GNP/GNP(-4))-1)*100*

An error occurs since GNP(-4) requires data between 1964:1 and 1964:4 to generate year-to-year percentage changes between 1965:1 and 1965:4.

A more serious error would occur if data are entered over the 1965:1 to 1983:4 period and then stored over a shorter sample period in effect when the *STORE* command is entered.

For example, if the *STORE* command is entered when the current sample period is set between 1980:1 and 1980:4, data will be stored over the 1980:1 to 1980:4 period, not the 1965:1 to 1983:4 period that may be desired.   This points to the importance of checking or resetting the sample period before entering the *STORE* command.

3.1-3.   (a)   Pros: Easy to understand and not distorted by seasonal changes.
                 Cons: Lack of symmetry and loss of four data points in quarterly calculations.
          (b)   Pros: Easy to understand and loss of only one observation in the calculation.
                 Cons: Lack of symmetry and the presence of seasonality in quarterly calculations.
          (c)   Pros: Symmetrical, a midpoint estimate and loss of only one observation in the calculation.
                 Cons: Not widely accepted or understood and the presence of seasonality in quarterly calculations.

3.1-4.   Since the prime interest rate is a short-term rate, the adjustment procedure described at the beginning of Computer Session 3.1-4 will be used since price changes over a short period are relevant in generating a real prime interest rate.

5

The real mortgage rate, on the other hand, is a long-term rate and, as a result, the second adjustment procedure described in Computer Session 3.1-4 is relevant in generating a real rate. The reason for this is that long-term price anticipations are more likely to be influenced by inflation rates over a longer period of time in the past.

Computer Exercises:

3.1-5.   Start-up the system using the *CREATE* command and then *FETCH* the Chicago employment data from the data disk.

>*FETCH NTO1 NMI1 NCN1 NMN1 NTR1 NWR1 NFI1 NSR1 NGV1*

Generate the total employment series (GNTO1). Print the newly generated total employment series (GNTO1) and the total included in the data disk (NTO1).

>*GENR GNTO1=NMI1+NCN1+NMN1+NTR1+NWR1+NFI1+NSR1+NGV1*
>*PRINT GNTO1 NTO1*

The two printed series should be the same.

3.1-6.   Print out the disposable income series (DSY) and compare it with the data for DSY in Appendix 2.

>*PRINT DSY*

3.1-7.   >*FETCH NTO1*
>*SMPL 66.1 83.4*
>*GENR PNTO1=((NTO1/NTO1(-4))-1)*100*
>*SMPL 65.2 83.4*
>*GENR CNTO1=((NTO1/NTO1(-1))^4-1)*100*
>*SMPL 66.1 83.4*
>*GENR LNTO1=(LOG(NTO1/NTO1(-4)))*100*
>*SMPL 65.1 83.4*
>*PRINT NTO1 PNTO1 CNTO1 LNTO1*

obs	NTO1	PNTO1	CNTO1	LNTO1
1965.1	2600300.	NA	NA	NA
1965.2	2681400.	NA	13.07135	NA
1965.3	2728100.	NA	7.150629	NA
1965.4	2781900.	NA	8.124700	NA
1966.1	2738700.	5.322463	-6.068385	5.185653
1966.2	2820300.	5.180130	12.46137	5.050422

1966.3	2870700.	5.227081	7.342080	5.095051
1966.4	2922700.	5.061289	7.444879	4.937370
1967.1	2851400.	4.115091	-9.406796	4.032675
1967.2	2899700.	2.815303	6.949730	2.776402
1967.3	2946500.	2.640471	6.613821	2.606212
1967.4	2962700.	1.368598	2.217423	1.359317
1968.1	2905900.	1.911342	-7.450954	1.893305
1968.2	2962200.	2.155395	7.977893	2.132495
1968.3	2989600.	1.462752	3.751606	1.452157
1968.4	3017200.	1.839538	3.744255	1.822823
1969.1	2966600.	2.088854	-6.541335	2.067336
1969.2	3024900.	2.116670	8.095625	2.094580
1969.3	3057900.	2.284587	4.435711	2.258881
1969.4	3057800.	1.345618	-0.013080	1.336645
1970.1	2981900.	0.515742	-9.565114	0.514417
1970.2	2976500.	-1.600053	-0.722405	-1.612992
1970.3	3005000.	-1.729945	3.885362	-1.745084
1970.4	2987100.	-2.312120	-2.361490	-2.339269
1971.1	2899000.	-2.780107	-11.28566	-2.819483
1971.2	2945900.	-1.028053	6.629934	-1.033374
1971.3	2969000.	-1.198003	3.173649	-1.205237
1971.4	2962500.	-0.823541	-0.872844	-0.826951
1972.1	2899700.	0.024146	-8.213494	0.024143
1972.2	2960400.	0.492209	8.639888	0.491002
1972.3	2990700.	0.730886	4.157326	0.728228
1972.4	2993900.	1.059916	0.428681	1.054338
1973.1	2953500.	1.855364	-5.289367	1.838362
1973.2	3041400.	2.736117	12.44658	2.699354
1973.3	3081100.	3.022704	5.324404	2.977920
1973.4	3109000.	3.844484	3.671579	3.772425
1974.1	3056700.	3.494160	-6.560957	3.434500
1974.2	3109500.	2.239101	7.090508	2.214401
1974.3	3126100.	1.460517	2.152552	1.449955
1974.4	3117600.	0.276616	-1.083189	0.276234
1975.1	2981400.	-2.463441	-16.36281	-2.494291
1975.2	2970500.	-4.470172	-1.454400	-4.573165
1975.3	2973000.	-4.897476	0.337069	-5.021468
1975.4	2987700.	-4.166667	1.992517	-4.255961
1976.1	2931900.	-1.660294	-7.263935	-1.674231
1976.2	2987900.	0.585760	7.861789	0.584051
1976.3	3049000.	2.556341	8.433996	2.524212
1976.4	3045500.	1.934599	-0.458377	1.916123
1977.1	2960500.	0.975477	-10.70527	0.970750
1977.2	3063600.	2.533552	14.67480	2.501990
1977.3	3082400.	1.095441	2.477316	1.089485
1977.4	3115500.	2.298473	4.365039	2.272456
1978.1	3063100.	3.465631	-6.559817	3.406930

7

1978.2	3129500.	2.151064	8.956996	2.128255
1978.3	3181200.	3.205295	6.773646	3.154997
1978.4	3183800.	2.192265	0.327322	2.168580
1979.1	3143300.	2.618263	-4.991991	2.584573
1979.2	3212400.	2.648985	9.087538	2.614507
1979.3	3241900.	1.908085	3.724175	1.890109
1979.4	3257800.	2.324267	1.976292	2.297667
1980.1	3195500.	1.660675	-7.432697	1.647037
1980.2	3228800.	0.510522	4.233973	0.509223
1980.3	3233800.	-0.249854	0.620866	-0.250166
1980.4	3223600.	-1.049788	-1.255717	-1.055337
1981.1	3169900.	-0.801127	-6.498698	-0.804353
1981.2	3192400.	-1.127354	2.869579	-1.133757
1981.3	3182100.	-1.598738	-1.284333	-1.611656
1981.4	3169700.	-1.672044	-1.549632	-1.686180
1982.1	3094500.	-2.378624	-9.157452	-2.407370
1982.2	3097800.	-2.963288	0.427246	-3.008080
1982.3	3085400.	-3.038874	-1.591548	-3.086005
1982.4	3044100.	-3.962520	-5.247700	-4.043166
1983.1	3110300.	0.510583	8.986690	0.509284
1983.2	3155600.	1.865840	5.954320	1.848647
1983.3	3213000.	4.135606	7.476895	4.052377
1983.4	3227500.	6.024769	1.817423	5.850256

==

3.1-8.

>*FETCH PDE PRR MTR*

[Perform the procedures described in Computer Session 3.1-4 for extending the price deflator (PDE) back to 1961:1.]

>*SMPL 65,1 83,4*
>*GENR PPDE16=((((PDE-PDE(-16))/ABS(PDE(-16)))+1)^(1/4)-1)*100*
>*GENR PPDE=((PDE-PDE(-4))/ABS(PDE(-4)))*100*
>*GENR RMTR=MTR-PPDE16*
>*GENR RPRR=PRR-PPDE*
>*PRINT PRR RPRR MTR RMTR*

==

obs	PRR	RPRR	MTR	RMTR
1965.1	4.500000	2.240510	5.977000	4.420359
1965.2	4.500000	2.223510	5.927000	4.246685
1965.3	4.500000	1.559236	5.927000	4.110561
1965.4	4.640000	2.375332	5.983000	4.143848
1966.1	5.117000	2.487204	6.063000	3.995685
1966.2	5.507000	2.201993	6.277000	4.136640
1966.3	5.877000	2.617874	6.560000	4.312253

8

1966.4	6.000000	2.278017	6.747000	4.331351
1967.1	5.807000	2.452087	6.643000	4.157222
1967.2	5.500000	2.953641	6.417000	3.846895
1967.3	5.500000	2.525590	6.447000	3.791656
1967.4	5.727000	2.665905	6.570000	3.809316
1968.1	6.000000	2.293932	6.710000	3.724023
1968.2	6.400000	1.803035	6.947000	3.769707
1968.3	6.467000	1.976585	7.247000	3.832747
1968.4	6.267000	1.449825	7.220000	3.757991
1969.1	7.063000	2.355673	7.410000	3.813172
1969.2	7.743000	2.921961	7.690000	3.876869
1969.3	8.500000	2.886774	8.023000	3.943996
1969.4	8.500000	2.987440	8.173000	3.899118
1970.1	8.463000	2.672721	8.377000	3.991654
1970.2	8.000000	2.227640	8.347000	3.919472
1970.3	7.943000	3.028148	8.400000	3.906262
1970.4	7.233000	2.256698	8.310000	3.722290
1971.1	5.883000	0.865753	7.827000	3.024436
1971.2	5.390000	0.305999	7.473000	2.405334
1971.3	5.967000	0.813935	7.700000	2.657895
1971.4	5.543000	0.856337	7.693000	2.695294
1972.1	4.893000	0.316727	7.500000	2.478273
1972.2	5.007000	1.119855	7.457000	2.568043
1972.3	5.340000	1.475511	7.523000	2.638557
1972.4	5.757000	1.495779	7.577000	2.718800
1973.1	6.107000	1.822156	7.697000	2.781372
1973.2	7.033000	1.671903	7.753000	2.729201
1973.3	9.130000	2.865668	8.037000	2.991276
1973.4	9.813000	2.722208	8.563000	3.314870
1974.1	9.257000	1.709645	8.657000	3.308421
1974.2	10.93700	2.602877	8.703000	3.048989
1974.3	11.99300	2.709234	9.153000	3.030359
1974.4	11.00300	0.841140	9.563000	3.038528
1975.1	8.980000	-2.002661	9.403000	2.589214
1975.2	7.323000	-2.335095	9.067000	2.281567
1975.3	7.563000	-1.249927	9.113000	2.078770
1975.4	7.583000	-0.097097	9.250000	1.972063
1976.1	6.833000	0.941075	9.207000	2.058838
1976.2	6.900000	1.387308	9.030000	1.829271
1976.3	7.087000	2.184890	9.090000	1.789444
1976.4	6.543000	1.891472	9.103000	1.724804
1977.1	6.250000	1.116278	8.993000	1.627454
1977.2	6.470000	0.597948	8.957000	1.626537
1977.3	6.903000	0.777630	9.040000	1.774540
1977.4	7.673000	1.561438	9.093000	1.961114
1978.1	7.977000	1.895130	9.197000	2.199089
1978.2	8.300000	1.192601	9.400000	2.374676

9

1978.3	9.140000	1.347332	9.747000	2.849318
1978.4	10.81000	2.334713	9.983000	3.263537
1979.1	11.75000	2.461139	10.39700	3.809693
1979.2	11.71700	3.012584	10.61700	3.825135
1979.3	12.11700	3.499710	11.09000	4.240399
1979.4	15.08000	6.925795	11.56300	4.726260
1980.1	16.39700	7.985897	12.53000	5.314341
1980.2	16.32300	7.296121	13.67300	6.002832
1980.3	11.61000	2.453027	12.41300	4.496035
1980.4	16.73300	6.569360	13.17300	4.956421
1981.1	19.21300	8.808209	14.07000	5.535030
1981.2	18.93000	9.806119	14.67000	6.182423
1981.3	20.32300	11.05757	15.58300	6.876476
1981.4	17.01300	8.321804	16.14300	7.274631
1982.1	16.27000	9.142569	15.76700	6.965578
1982.2	16.50000	9.442459	15.89000	7.415050
1982.3	14.71700	9.085841	15.46000	7.302581
1982.4	11.95700	7.593628	14.39700	6.575333
1983.1	10.88000	6.223241	13.33000	5.700229
1983.2	10.50000	6.425303	12.79000	5.488955
1983.3	10.79700	6.754313	12.73300	5.732831
1983.4	11.00000	6.871419	12.54000	5.735961

===

>*SMPL 61.1 83.4*
>*PRINT PDE PPDE PPDE16*

==

obs	PDE	PPDE	PPDE16
1961.1	0.693500	NA	NA
1961.2	0.693500	NA	NA
1961.3	0.693800	NA	NA
1961.4	0.696900	NA	NA
1962.1	0.697600	NA	NA
1962.2	0.703600	NA	NA
1962.3	0.704400	NA	NA
1962.4	0.706700	NA	NA
1963.1	0.709300	NA	NA
1963.2	0.709500	NA	NA
1963.3	0.713900	NA	NA
1963.4	0.718600	NA	NA
1964.1	0.721400	NA	NA
1964.2	0.724800	NA	NA
1964.3	0.724300	NA	NA
1964.4	0.733000	NA	NA
1965.1	0.737700	2.259490	1.556641

1965.2	0.741300	2.276490	1.680315
1965.3	0.745600	2.940764	1.816439
1965.4	0.749600	2.264668	1.839152
1966.1	0.757100	2.629796	2.067315
1966.2	0.765800	3.305007	2.140360
1966.3	0.769900	3.259126	2.247747
1966.4	0.777500	3.721983	2.415649
1967.1	0.782500	3.354913	2.485778
1967.2	0.785300	2.546359	2.570105
1967.3	0.792800	2.974410	2.655344
1967.4	0.801300	3.061095	2.760684
1968.1	0.811500	3.706068	2.985977
1968.2	0.821400	4.596965	3.177293
1968.3	0.828400	4.490415	3.414253
1968.4	0.839900	4.817175	3.462009
1969.1	0.849700	4.707327	3.596828
1969.2	0.861000	4.821039	3.813131
1969.3	0.874900	5.613226	4.079004
1969.4	0.886200	5.512560	4.273882
1970.1	0.898900	5.790279	4.385346
1970.2	0.910700	5.772360	4.427528
1970.3	0.917900	4.914852	4.493737
1970.4	0.930300	4.976302	4.587711
1971.1	0.944000	5.017247	4.802564
1971.2	0.957000	5.084001	5.067666
1971.3	0.965200	5.153065	5.042105
1971.4	0.973900	4.686663	4.997706
1972.1	0.987200	4.576273	5.021727
1972.2	0.994200	3.887145	4.888957
1972.3	1.002500	3.864489	4.884443
1972.4	1.015400	4.261221	4.858200
1973.1	1.029500	4.284844	4.915628
1973.2	1.047500	5.361097	5.023799
1973.3	1.065300	6.264332	5.045724
1973.4	1.087400	7.090792	5.248130
1974.1	1.107200	7.547355	5.348579
1974.2	1.134800	8.334124	5.654011
1974.3	1.164200	9.283766	6.122641
1974.4	1.197900	10.16186	6.524472
1975.1	1.228800	10.98266	6.813786
1975.2	1.244400	9.658095	6.785434
1975.3	1.266800	8.812927	7.034230
1975.4	1.289900	7.680097	7.277937
1976.1	1.301200	5.891925	7.148162
1976.2	1.313000	5.512692	7.200729
1976.3	1.328900	4.902110	7.300556
1976.4	1.349900	4.651528	7.378196

1977.1	1.368000	5.133722	7.365546
1977.2	1.390100	5.872052	7.330463
1977.3	1.410300	6.125370	7.265460
1977.4	1.432400	6.111562	7.131886
1978.1	1.451200	6.081870	6.997911
1978.2	1.488900	7.107399	7.025324
1978.3	1.520200	7.792668	6.897682
1978.4	1.553800	8.475287	6.719463
1979.1	1.586000	9.288861	6.587307
1979.2	1.618500	8.704416	6.791865
1979.3	1.651200	8.617290	6.849601
1979.4	1.680500	8.154205	6.836740
1980.1	1.719400	8.411102	7.215659
1980.2	1.764600	9.026879	7.670168
1980.3	1.802400	9.156973	7.916965
1980.4	1.851300	10.16364	8.216579
1981.1	1.898300	10.40479	8.534969
1981.2	1.925600	9.123881	8.487577
1981.3	1.969400	9.265427	8.706524
1981.4	2.012200	8.691196	8.868369
1982.1	2.033600	7.127432	8.801422
1982.2	2.061500	7.057541	8.474951
1982.3	2.080300	5.631159	8.157419
1982.4	2.100000	4.363372	7.821667
1983.1	2.128300	4.656759	7.629771
1983.2	2.145500	4.074697	7.301045
1983.3	2.164400	4.042687	7.000169
1983.4	2.186700	4.128581	6.804039

==

>*SAVE CE3-1-8*

Study Projects:

3.1-9.

>*FETCH NWR1*
>*SEAS(M) NWR1 SNWR1*
Generate Factor Series? (Y/N) N
>*PRINT SNWR1 NWR1*

obs	SNWR1	NWR1
1965.1	570795.1	562600.0
1965.2	577030.2	576100.0
1965.3	587098.1	584200.0
1965.4	600736.9	613500.0
1966.1	597579.7	589000.0

12

1966.2	607579.4	606600.0
1966.3	616442.9	613400.0
1966.4	630896.1	644300.0
1967.1	623248.3	614300.0
1967.2	630115.8	629100.0
1967.3	636240.7	633100.0
1967.4	643527.8	657200.0
1968.1	644351.2	635100.0
1968.2	648745.8	647700.0
1968.3	651214.6	648000.0
1968.4	662132.4	676200.0
1969.1	660685.8	651200.0
1969.2	661366.1	660300.0
1969.3	663977.6	660700.0
1969.4	671532.8	685800.0
1970.1	671744.5	662100.0
1970.2	661265.9	660200.0
1970.3	661063.2	657800.0
1970.4	662720.0	676800.0
1971.1	661700.3	652200.0
1971.2	660765.1	659700.0
1971.3	666289.0	663000.0
1971.4	667909.8	682100.0
1972.1	665352.8	655800.0
1972.2	663469.5	662400.0
1972.3	661867.2	658600.0
1972.4	656942.8	670900.0
1973.1	659265.3	649800.0
1973.2	671181.9	670100.0
1973.3	680358.4	677000.0
1973.4	689745.8	704400.0
1974.1	694369.3	684400.0
1974.2	698225.6	697100.0
1974.3	707090.4	703600.0
1974.4	702671.2	717600.0
1975.1	695383.9	685400.0
1975.2	681899.3	680800.0
1975.3	677645.1	674300.0
1975.4	688962.4	703600.0
1976.1	696905.8	686900.0
1976.2	700228.8	699100.0
1976.3	705984.9	702500.0
1976.4	707567.2	722600.0
1977.1	697007.2	687000.0
1977.2	717857.2	716700.0
1977.3	717542.0	714000.0
1977.4	724115.6	739500.0

13

1978.1	733633.1	723100.0
1978.2	745401.6	744200.0
1978.3	743269.0	739600.0
1978.4	737726.4	753400.0
1979.1	746213.7	735500.0
1979.2	756419.4	755200.0
1979.3	756333.5	752600.0
1979.4	763968.9	780200.0
1980.1	777665.3	766500.0
1980.2	774348.3	773100.0
1980.3	769598.9	765800.0
1980.4	762010.5	778200.0
1981.1	767418.1	756400.0
1981.2	761126.9	759900.0
1981.3	761458.8	757700.0
1981.4	755645.7	771700.0
1982.1	759301.6	748400.0
1982.2	747605.1	746400.0
1982.3	746484.9	742800.0
1982.4	729892.8	745400.0
1983.1	763178.4	752221.1
1983.2	761554.3	760326.6
1983.3	777356.6	773519.3
1983.4	773867.2	790308.6

================================

>*SAVE SP3-1-9*

3.1-10.   >*FETCH GNP CUN INR IRE INV GEX GSL EXT IMP*

[Compute a temporary variable for GNP:]

>*GENR TGNP=CUN+INR+IRE+INV+GEX+GSL+EXT−IMP*
>*PRINT GNP TGNP*

================================

obs	GNP	TGNP
1965.1	668.8000	727.0000
1965.2	681.7000	740.2000
1965.3	696.4000	759.2000
1965.4	717.2000	780.0000
1966.1	738.5000	804.8001
1966.2	750.0000	817.0000
1966.3	760.6000	830.5000
1966.4	774.9000	848.0000
1967.1	780.7000	857.0000

14

1967.2	788.6000	865.5000
1967.3	805.7000	884.3000
1967.4	823.3000	904.2000
1968.1	841.2000	924.3000
1968.2	867.2000	955.5000
1968.3	884.9000	975.4000
1968.4	900.3000	993.4000
1969.1	921.2000	1015.200
1969.2	937.4000	1034.800
1969.3	955.3000	1054.700
1969.4	962.0000	1064.900
1970.1	972.0000	1076.100
1970.2	986.3000	1106.600
1970.3	1003.600	1124.400
1970.4	1009.000	1134.500
1971.1	1049.300	1178.000
1971.2	1068.900	1206.400
1971.3	1086.600	1225.000
1971.4	1105.800	1246.500
1972.1	1142.400	1289.000
1972.2	1171.700	1326.300
1972.3	1196.100	1347.300
1972.4	1233.500	1405.400
1973.1	1283.500	1454.500
1973.2	1307.600	1483.300
1973.3	1337.700	1514.300
1973.4	1376.700	1555.100
1974.1	1387.700	1574.200
1974.2	1423.800	1620.200
1974.3	1451.600	1655.800
1974.4	1473.800	1686.100
1975.1	1479.800	1708.100
1975.2	1516.700	1764.800
1975.3	1578.500	1835.800
1975.4	1621.800	1884.000
1976.1	1672.000	1939.100
1976.2	1698.600	1966.100
1976.3	1729.000	2005.500
1976.4	1772.000	2057.000
1977.1	1834.800	2119.700
1977.2	1895.100	2184.800
1977.3	1954.400	2257.300
1977.4	1988.900	2299.600
1978.1	2031.700	2349.200
1978.2	2139.500	2461.300
1978.3	2202.500	2531.000
1978.4	2281.600	2619.900

1979.1	2335.500	2675.100
1979.2	2377.900	2724.300
1979.3	2454.800	2819.800
1979.4	2502.900	2879.600
1980.1	2572.900	2964.200
1980.2	2578.800	2982.000
1980.3	2639.100	3076.000
1980.4	2736.000	3184.100
1981.1	2866.600	3338.100
1981.2	2912.500	3386.800
1981.3	3004.900	3496.400
1981.4	3032.200	3530.600
1982.1	3021.400	3525.600
1982.2	3070.200	3579.100
1982.3	3090.700	3609.600
1982.4	3109.600	3663.800
1983.1	3171.500	3718.400
1983.2	3272.000	3829.500
1983.3	3362.200	3920.600
1983.4	3437.300	4029.400

================================

Since government expenditures (GEX and GSL) include social security payments as well as other transfer payments, double counting occurs since these payments are used to fund other expenditures. It is the expenditure rather than the transfer payment that results in the production of a good or service.

Government purchases (GPF and GPS) rather than government expenditures should be included in the GNP equation since "purchases" are defined to include final goods and services purchased by the government and, therefore, do not include transfer payments.

3.1-11. Follow the procedures presented in Computer Session 3.1-4.

>*CREATE*
Frequency? *Q*
Starting date? *61.1*
Ending date? *83.4*
>*DATA CPI*

[Using the data editor, enter the following CPI data]

obs		CPI		
1961	89.40000	89.36000	89.73000	89.85000
1962	90.20000	90.53000	90.79000	91.02000
1963	91.29000	91.46000	92.02000	92.29000
1964	92.66000	92.81000	93.00000	93.43000
1965	93.72000	94.33000	94.64000	95.10000
1966	96.00000	96.89000	97.71000	98.51000
1967	98.83000	99.37000	100.3700	101.3700
1968	102.4700	103.4300	104.7300	106.1300
1969	107.4000	109.1000	110.6000	112.2300
1970	114.0700	115.7000	116.9700	118.5300
1971	119.5700	120.8000	121.9700	122.6700
1972	123.8700	124.6300	125.6700	126.9700
1973	128.9330	131.5660	134.1660	137.5660
1974	141.7010	145.4000	149.5330	154.3010
1975	157.5000	159.2330	162.5330	165.7340
1976	167.5000	168.8340	171.5330	174.1670
1977	177.3000	180.4330	182.9000	185.5670
1978	188.9000	193.2000	197.5330	202.3000
1979	207.4660	213.7670	220.7340	228.1330
1980	237.0000	244.6330	249.1670	256.8000
1981	263.5660	268.5660	276.1670	281.3990
1982	283.6000	286.8000	292.1000	293.9670
1983	293.5330	296.5670	300.0330	303.5670

```
>FETCH AAA CPI
>SMPL 65.1 83.4
>GENR PCPI=((CPI-CPI(-4))/ABS(CPI(-4)))*100
>GENR RAAA=AAA-PCPI
>PRINT RAAA
```

obs		RAAA		
1965	3.276035	2.805241	2.733560	2.825568
1966	2.380223	2.289126	2.076129	1.797297
1967	2.172081	2.703393	2.894655	3.123741
1968	2.443909	2.167262	1.733072	1.547336
1969	1.888836	1.405033	1.458116	1.719326
1970	1.682574	2.090505	2.460504	2.293532
1971	2.395399	3.065043	3.282399	3.807214
1972	3.636778	4.106475	4.173470	3.631658
1973	3.132654	1.741729	0.826435	-0.695273
1974	-2.005822	-2.151870	-2.466719	-3.148069

17

1975	-2.442531	-0.640760	0.219267	1.400457
1976	2.220794	2.503472	2.925664	3.094717
1977	2.182252	1.142939	1.320293	1.557562
1978	1.907422	1.594244	0.752447	0.009771
1979	-0.535486	-1.255449	-2.455370	-2.226640
1980	-2.092581	-3.236080	-1.304120	0.264090
1981	1.953711	4.199768	4.083901	5.037950
1982	7.408869	7.720616	7.983659	7.410735
1983	8.340538	8.164491	9.627155	9.144336

===

>*SMPL 65.1 83.4*
>*GENR PCPI16=((((CPI-CPI(-16))/ABS(CPI(-16)))+1)^(1/4)-1)*100*
>*GENR RAAA=AAA-PCPI16*
>*PRINT RAAAR*

===

obs		RAAAR		
1965	3.233240	3.080650	3.156216	3.183191
1966	3.242830	3.291137	3.466667	3.386357
1967	3.116189	3.167635	3.421816	3.653229
1968	3.579257	3.507469	3.062812	3.005388
1969	3.235110	3.183426	3.090114	3.239549
1970	3.487098	3.604549	3.619474	3.173169
1971	2.339251	2.469709	2.563534	2.416487
1972	2.377226	2.505294	2.544737	2.552881
1973	2.545728	2.514614	2.639563	2.429459
1974	2.324606	2.484505	2.654595	2.201295
1975	1.576142	1.723158	1.471483	0.997700
1976	0.734398	0.648431	0.374617	-0.039159
1977	-0.256455	-0.203400	-0.107486	0.333116
1978	0.997938	1.305506	1.545381	2.021330
1979	2.161646	1.749207	1.337697	2.226623
1980	3.078507	1.488562	1.793844	2.636170
1981	2.743660	3.528410	4.069020	3.647039
1982	4.317400	4.129340	3.479040	2.083741
1983	2.779986	3.041066	4.367569	5.006951

===

3.2 Exercises

Questions for Review:

3.2-1. While a plot represents movements in one or more series over time, a scatter diagram represents the joint relationship between two variables.

18

3.2-2.   When the relationship between two variables is of greater interest than how variables move over time, a scatter diagram is a more relevant graphical tool than a plot. For example, the relationship between sales and advertising expenditures may be of particular interest when the effectiveness of an advertising campaign is being evaluated. Hence, in this example, a scatter diagram between sales and advertising would probably be a more useful descriptive tool than a plot.

3.2-3.   As explained in Section 3.1, the selection of a base year is critical in calculating the annual percentage change. When percentage changes approach zero, the differences are small. In such a case, the selection of a base year will not be critical since the values at the beginning and end of a period (alternative bases) will be roughly the same.

3.2-4.   If two series move together in a one-to-one relationship and both started at a level of 2,000 and one grew at a ten percent rate while the other grew at a five percent rate, the resulting levels of 3,200 and 2,100 will follow a relatively straight line. The resulting two-to-one rate of growth (10 percent to 5 percent), however, will deviate markedly from a linear path in a scatter diagram of the two series measured in percentage change form.

3.2-5.   The short-run Phillips Curve shows an inverse relationship between the rate of change in money wages and the rate of employment. In the long-run, the inverse relationship tends to break down resulting in a series of looped paths.

3.2-6.   A scatter diagram showing the relationship between government spending deficits and interest rates may shed light on this issue. The "crowding-out" thesis suggests an inverse relationship exists between spending deficits and interest rates.

3.2-7.   A plot could be constructed showing the ratio of local employment to U.S. employment over some time interval.

Computer Exercises:

3.2-8.   Compute the ratio of Chicago total wage and salary employment (NTO1) to non-agricultural employment in the U.S. (NUS). Before finding the ratio, notice that the unit of measurement should be changed.

```
>FETCH NTO1 NUS
>GENR TNUS=NUS*1000
>GENR TNTO1=NTO1/1000
>GENR RATIO=TNTO1/TNUS
>PLOT(A) RATIO
```

19

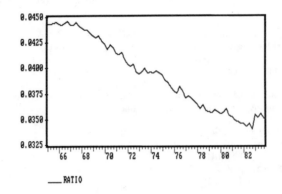

_____ RATIO

3.2-9.

```
>FETCH NTO1 GNP PDE
>GENR RGNP=GNP/PDE
>SMPL 66.1 83.4
>GENR PRGNP=((RGNP/RGNP(-4))-1)*100
>GENR PNTO1=((NTO1/NTO1(-4))-1)*100
>PLOT(A) PRGNP PNTO1
```

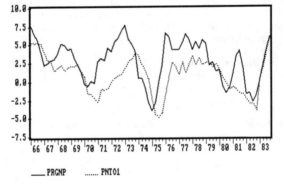

_____ PRGNP PNTO1

The result shows that the year-to-year percentage changes in total employment in Chicago follow (lags) year-to-year percentage changes in
RGNP by about 3 or 4 quarters.

3.2-10.   Plot and graph the federal government spending deficit and the real interest rate.   Since the deficit is shown in billions of dollars and the
interest rate is in percentages, use the normalized scaling method when
plotting.

20

```
>FETCH GEX TFG PRR PDE
>SMPL 66.1 83.4
>GENR PPDE=((PDE-PDE(-4))/ABS(PDE(-4)))*100
>GENR RPRR=PRR-PPDE
>GENR DEF=GEX-TFG
>PLOT(N) DEF RPRR
```

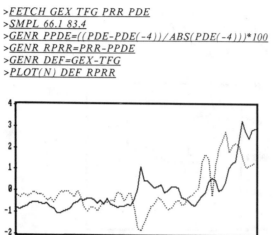

```
___ DEF      ....... RPRR
```

```
>GRAPH RPRR DEF
```

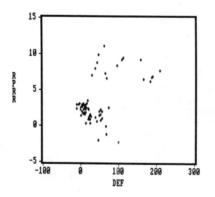

The plot and graph suggest that higher deficits are more closely associated with lower rather than higher real interest rates.

21

3.2-11.

> *>FETCH NTO1 GNP PDE*
> *>GENR RGNP=GNP/PDE*
> *>GRAPH NTO1 RGNP*

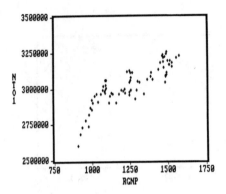

> *>SMPL 65.4 83.4*
> *>GENR ANTO1=(NTO1+NTO1(-1)+NTO1(-2)+NTO1(-3))/4*
> *>GENR ARGNP=(RGNP+RGNP(-1)+RGNP(-2)+RGNP(-3))/4*
> *>PRINT ANTO1 ARGNP*

obs	ANTO1	ARGNP
1965.4	2697925.	929.2481
1966.1	2732525.	946.4558
1966.2	2767250.	961.3976
1966.3	2802900.	974.8745
1966.4	2838100.	984.8442
1967.1	2866275.	990.4110
1967.2	2886125.	996.6196
1967.3	2905075.	1003.707
1967.4	2915075.	1011.407
1968.1	2928700.	1021.132
1968.2	2944325.	1034.021
1968.3	2955100.	1047.004
1968.4	2968725.	1058.119
1969.1	2983900.	1070.006
1969.2	2999575.	1078.250
1969.3	3016650.	1084.172
1969.4	3026800.	1087.578
1970.1	3030625.	1086.872

22

1970.2	3018525.	1085.441
1970.3	3005300.	1085.808
1970.4	2987625.	1085.574
1971.1	2966900.	1093.130
1971.2	2959250.	1101.609
1971.3	2950250.	1109.712
1971.4	2944100.	1122.422
1972.1	2944275.	1133.838
1972.2	2947900.	1149.240
1972.3	2953325.	1166.075
1972.4	2961175.	1185.914
1973.1	2974625.	1208.292
1973.2	2994875.	1225.734
1973.3	3017475.	1241.380
1973.4	3046250.	1254.194
1974.1	3072050.	1255.849
1974.2	3089075.	1257.441
1974.3	3100325.	1255.231
1974.4	3102475.	1246.300
1975.1	3083650.	1234.030
1975.2	3048900.	1225.067
1975.3	3010625.	1224.864
1975.4	2978150.	1231.611
1976.1	2965775.	1251.787
1976.2	2970125.	1270.502
1976.3	2989125.	1284.258
1976.4	3003575.	1298.103
1977.1	3010725.	1312.168
1977.2	3029650.	1329.569
1977.3	3038000.	1350.751
1977.4	3055500.	1369.706
1978.1	3081150.	1384.402
1978.2	3097625.	1402.823
1978.3	3122325.	1418.578
1978.4	3139400.	1438.551
1979.1	3159450.	1456.691
1979.2	3180175.	1464.749
1979.3	3195350.	1474.212
1979.4	3213850.	1479.457
1980.1	3226900.	1485.412
1980.2	3231000.	1483.464
1980.3	3228975.	1477.849
1980.4	3220425.	1474.974
1981.1	3214025.	1478.397
1981.2	3204925.	1491.175
1981.3	3192000.	1506.570
1981.4	3178525.	1513.827

1982.1	3159675.	1507.740
1982.2	3136025.	1501.937
1982.3	3111850.	1491.913
1982.4	3080450.	1485.376
1983.1	3084400.	1486.480
1983.2	3098850.	1495.417
1983.3	3130750.	1512.345
1983.4	3176600.	1535.133

================================

The fourth quarter figures represent the annual average for each year. Begin a new session by specifying the use of annual data during start-up.

>*DATA ANTO1 ARGNP*

[Enter the fourth quarter figures for ANTO1 and ARGNP shown above]

>*PRINT ANTO1 ARGNP*

================================

obs	ANTO1	ARGNP
1965	2697925.	929.2481
1966	2838100.	984.8442
1967	2915075.	1011.407
1968	2968725.	1058.119
1969	3026800.	1087.578
1970	2987625.	1085.574
1971	2944100.	1122.422
1972	2961175.	1185.914
1973	3046250.	1254.194
1974	3102475.	1246.300
1975	2978150.	1231.611
1976	3003575.	1298.103
1977	3055500.	1369.706
1978	3139400.	1438.551
1979	3213850.	1479.457
1980	3220425.	1474.974
1981	3178525.	1513.827
1982	3080450.	1485.376
1983	3176600.	1535.133

================================

>*GRAPH ANTO1 ARGNP*

24

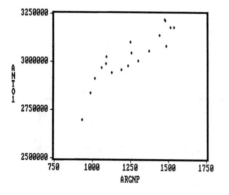

>*SAVE CE3-2-11*

3-2-12.   >*FETCH PDE UNP*
>*SMPL 66.1 83.4*
>*GENR PPDE=((PDE-PDE(-4))/ABS(PDE(-4)))*100*
>*GRAPH(C) PPDE UNP*

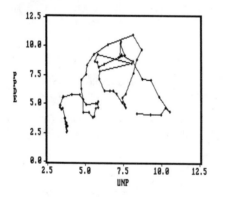

The graph shows a series of looped paths rather than the stable nega-
tively slopped curve implied by the Phillips trade-off. This results from
the fact that workers' wages initially fall behind inflation. As a result,
workers try to catch-up by demanding wage increases in excess of expected price increases. This process causes higher inflationary expecta-
tions which is shown by the upswing in the looped pattern.

Study Projects:

3.2-13.   >*LOAD SP3-1-9*
             >*PLOT(A) SNWR1 NWR1*

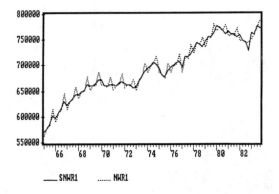

The seasonally adjusted series removes the seasonal fluctuations. As a result, the other components of time series data such as the trend and cyclical components are more clearly evident.

3.2-14.   *Note to Instructor:* The following sources may be helpful here:

Black, Fisher. "The ABC's of Business Cycles." *Financial Analysts Journal*, November-December 1981, pp. 75-80.

Dauten, Carl A. and Lloyd M. Valentine. *Business Cycles and Forecastin*g. Cincinnati: South Western Publishing Company, 1978.

Gordon, Robert A. *Business Fluctuations.* 2nd edition. New York: Harper and Row, 1961.

Moore, Geoffrey H. (editor) *Business Cycle Indicators Vol. 1.* Princeton: Princeton University Press, 1961.

Mitchell, W. C. "Business Cycles." In American Economic Association: *Readings in Business Cycle Theory.* New York: McGraw-Hill Book Company, 1944.

3.3 Exercises

Questions for Review:

3.3-1. Total dispersion is represented in the numerator as the sum of the differences of the x_t observations away from the mean. Since such a sum by definition is always equal to zero, the differences are squared before being summed. An average for the total dispersion is arrived at by dividing the numerator by the number of degrees of freedom in a series. The square root of this average measure of total dispersion is the standard deviation.

3.3-2. The coefficient of variation and correlation coefficient are relative rather than absolute measures of dispersion and association, respectively. Hence, unlike the standard deviation, the coefficient of variation can be used to compare the relative dispersion of two series measured in different units. Similarly, the fact that the correlation coefficient is a relative measure of dispersion means that it can be compared with other correlation coefficients to compare the degree of linear association between different series.

3.3-3. In regions II and IV, higher (lower) values than the mean in one series are associated with lower (higher) values than the mean in the other series.

3.3-4.

OBS.	NTO1	RGNP
1965:1	2,600,300	906.6
1965:2	2,681,400	919.6
1965:3	2,728,100	934.0
1965:4	2,781,900	956.8
1966:1	2,738,700	975.4
1966:2	2,820,300	979.4
1966:3	2,870,700	987.9
1966:4	2,922,700	996.7
Total	22,144,100	7,656.4

OBS.	$(NTO-\overline{NTO1})$	$(RGNP-\overline{RGNP})$	$(NTO-\overline{NTO1})(RGNP-\overline{RGNP})$
1965:1	-167,712.5	-50.4	8,452,710.00
1965:2	-86,612.5	-37.4	3,239,307.50
1965:3	-39,912.5	-23.0	917,987.50
1965:4	13,887.5	-0.2	-2,777.50
1966:1	-29,312.5	18.4	-539,350.00
1966:2	52,287.5	22.4	1,171,240.00
1966:3	102,687.5	30.9	3,173,043.75
1966:4	154,687.5	39.7	6,141,093.75
Total	-2*	0.4*	22,553,255.00

*Totals do not add to zero due to rounding error.

27

$$\overline{NTO1} = 2,768,012.5$$

$$\overline{RGNP} = 957.0$$

$$s_{NTO1} = 103,841.4$$

$$s_{RGNP} = 33.5$$

$$cov_{NTO1 \cdot RGNP} = 22,553,255/7 = 3,221,893.6$$

$$r_{NTO1 \cdot RGNP} = 3,221,893.6/(103,841.4)(33.5) = 0.93$$

3.3-5. a. $cov_{x \cdot y}$ is the population covariance while $\widehat{cov}_{x \cdot y}$ is the sample co-variance.
  b. ρ is the population correlation coefficient while r is the sample cor-relation coefficient.
  c. t_c is a critical t that is given or obtained from a table while t_m is a measured t based on a sample.
  d. z_c is a critical z that is given or obtained from a table while z_m is a measured z based on a sample.

3.3-6.

$$H_0: \rho = 0$$
$$H_1: \rho \neq 0$$

$$t_m = \frac{r\sqrt{n-2}}{\sqrt{1-r^2}} = \frac{0.93\sqrt{8-2}}{\sqrt{1-.93^2}} = 6.197$$

At a .05 level of significance and n-2 or 8-2 degrees of freedom, t_c = 2.447 for a two tailed test. Since 6.197 is greater than 2.447, H_0 is re-jected. A significant linear relationship exists.

3.3-7. The chances of incorrectly rejecting H_0 when it should have been accep-ted (Type I error) is slightly greater when a 0.10 rather than 0.05 level of significance (0.10 vs. 0.05) is used.

3.3-8. No. The covariance and correlation coefficient measure the linear pat-terns of association, not the causal relationships between variables.

Computer Exercises:

3.3-9.   >*FETCH EXT IMP*
      >*SMPL 65.1 83.4*
      >*COVA EXT IMP*

28

SMPL   1965.1 - 1983.4
76 Observations

===
Series	Mean	S.D.	Maximum	Minimum
===
| EXT | 163.74737 | 115.69543 | 371.00000 | 36.900000 |
| IMP | 154.35790 | 112.78073 | 371.00000 | 29.100000 |
===
| | | Covariance | Correlation | |
===
EXT,EXT		13209.308	1.0000000	
EXT,IMP		12818.487	0.9954926	
IMP,IMP		12552.131	1.0000000	
===

From the output:

$$cv_{ext} = (115.69543/163.74737)*100 = 70.65\%$$

$$cv_{imp} = (112.78073/154.35790)*100 = 73.06\%$$

Since $cv_{imp} > cv_{ext}$, there is a greater relative dispersion in the imports of goods and services than there is in the exports of goods and services.

3.3-10.   >*FETCH GNP PDE NMI1 NCN1 NMN1 NTR1 NWR1 NFI1 NSR1 NGV1*
>*GENR RGNP = GNP/PDE*
>*COVA RGNP NMI1 NCN1 NMN1 NTR1 NWR1 NFI1 NSR1 NGV1*

SMPL   1965.1 - 1983.4
76 Observations

===
Series	Mean	S.D.	Maximum	Minimum
===
RGNP	1252.2283	194.18649	1571.9120	906.60160
NMI1	4736.2376	907.00244	6699.9990	2599.9990
NCN1	114301.07	12881.808	141100.00	88000.000
NMN1	866787.67	90288.960	1001700.0	653700.00
NTR1	197607.35	7589.0328	211300.00	179300.00
NWR1	692616.79	55009.821	790308.60	562600.00
NFI1	198105.72	27718.668	255757.00	155400.00
NSR1	573530.51	89901.995	791733.60	418600.00
NGV1	380458.08	40327.124	429900.00	280200.00
===
| | | Covariance | Correlation | |
===
| RGNP,RGNP | | 37212.229 | 1.0000000 | |
| RGNP,NMI1 | | -126075.31 | -0.7253622 | |

29

RGNP,NCN1	-440478.97	-0.1784357
RGNP,NMN1	-14410979.	-0.8328987
RGNP,NTR1	-861690.88	-0.5925137
RGNP,NWR1	10083691.	0.9565609
RGNP,NFI1	5061374.2	0.9528607
RGNP,NSR1	16563124.	0.9614047
RGNP,NGV1	6708334.3	0.8680621
NMI1,NMI1	811829.04	1.0000000
NMI1,NCN1	3250996.6	0.2819574
NMI1,NMN1	63229206.	0.7823966
NMI1,NTR1	3490742.4	0.5138960
NMI1,NWR1	-33988004.	-0.6902864
NMI1,NFI1	-20015315.	-0.8067407
NMI1,NSR1	-64563083.	-0.8023407
NMI1,NGV1	-23087200.	-0.6396139
NCN1,NCN1	163757535	1.0000000
NCN1,NMN1	535381741	0.4664493
NCN1,NTR1	57922384.	0.6003929
NCN1,NWR1	-28006615.	-0.0400494
NCN1,NFI1	-72701315.	-0.2063219
NCN1,NSR1	-239327747	-0.2094109
NCN1,NGV1	-35746118.	-0.0697280
NMN1,NMN1	8.045D+09	1.0000000
NMN1,NTR1	560745608	0.8292722
NMN1,NWR1	-3.645D+09	-0.7436233
NMN1,NFI1	-2.171D+09	-0.8791997
NMN1,NSR1	-7.055D+09	-0.8806939
NMN1,NGV1	-2.510D+09	-0.6984876
NTR1,NTR1	56835610.	1.0000000
NTR1,NWR1	-187273752	-0.4545719
NTR1,NFI1	-121454779	-0.5850704
NTR1,NSR1	-411002941	-0.6104379
NTR1,NGV1	-149635459	-0.4954538
NWR1,NWR1	2.986D+09	1.0000000
NWR1,NFI1	1.395D+09	0.9267911
NWR1,NSR1	4.576D+09	0.9377116
NWR1,NGV1	1.889D+09	0.8629437
NFI1,NFI1	758215019	1.0000000
NFI1,NSR1	2.436D+09	0.9906181
NFI1,NGV1	840358704	0.7618113
NSR1,NSR1	7.976D+09	1.0000000
NSR1,NGV1	2.797D+09	0.7818673
NGV1,NGV1	1.605D+09	1.0000000

Use the correlation coefficients that correspond to RGNP and each of the Chicago employment series. The rest are irrelevant for our purpose.

30

$$H_0: \rho = 0$$
$$H_1: \rho \neq 0$$

At a 0.05 level of significance, the critical t value is 1.980. Therefore in each of the following cases, if $|t_m|$ is greater than 1.980, it is appropriate to conclude that the correlation between the variables is significantly different from zero.

<u>NMI1 and RGNP</u>:

$$r = -0.7253622$$

$$t_m = \frac{-0.7253622\sqrt{76 - 2}}{\sqrt{1 - .7253622}} = -11.907$$

$$|-11.907| > 1.980$$

H_0 is rejected and H_1 is accepted.

<u>NCN1 and RGNP</u>: $r = -0.1784357$; $t_m = -1.693$; $|-1.693| < 1.980$. H_0 is accepted and H_1 is rejected.

<u>NMN1 and RGNP</u>: $r = -0.8328987$; $t_m = -17.527$; $|-17.527| > 1.980$. H_0 is rejected and H_1 is accepted.

<u>NTR1 and RGNP</u>: $r = -0.5925137$; $t_m = -7.985$; $|-7.985| > 1.980$. H_0 is rejected and H_1 is accepted.

<u>NWR1 and RGNP</u>: $r = 0.9565609$; $t_m = 39.481$; $|39.481| > 1.980$ H_0 is rejected and H_1 is accepted.

<u>NFI1 and RGNP</u>: $r = 0.9528607$; $t_m = 37.753$; $|37.753| > 1.980$. H_0 is rejected and H_1 is accepted.

<u>NSR1 and RGNP</u>: $r = 0.9614047$; $t_m = 42.097$; $|42.097| > 1.980$. H_0 is rejected and H_1 is accepted.

<u>NGV1 and RGNP</u>: $r = 0.8680621$; $t_m = 20.558$; $|20.558| > 1.980$. H_0 is rejected and H_1 is accepted.

3.3-11.
```
>FETCH GEX GSL TFG TSL PRR PDE MNS
>SMPL 65.1 83.4
>GENR DEF=GEX-TFG
>GENR TDEF=(GEX+GSL)-(TFG+TSL)
>SMPL 66.1 83.4
>GENR PPDE=((PDE-PDE(-4))/ABS(PDE(-4))*100
>GENR RPRR=PRR-PPDE
>COVA DEF TDEF RPRR MNS
```

SMPL   1966.1 - 1983.4
72 Observations

Series	Mean	S.D.	Maximum	Minimum
DEF	41.518056	51.247715	208.30000	-11.399990
TDEF	24.943057	41.663817	175.40000	-22.199980
RPRR	3.1182863	2.9134253	11.057570	-2.3350950
MNS	299.70786	99.897810	523.30000	171.43300

	Covariance	Correlation
DEF,DEF	2589.8515	1.0000000
DEF,TDEF	2029.1545	0.9637307
DEF,RPRR	75.173854	0.5105786
DEF,MNS	4081.2738	0.8084244
TDEF,TDEF	1711.7643	1.0000000
TDEF,RPRR	47.421847	0.3961774
TDEF,MNS	2626.7430	0.6399952
RPRR,RPRR	8.3701574	1.0000000
RPRR,MNS	194.54323	0.6778450
MNS,MNS	9840.9674	1.0000000

Use the correlation coefficients that correspond to the relevant relationships.

$$H_0: \rho = 0$$
$$H_1: \rho \neq 0$$

At .05 level of significance $t_c = 1.980$.
At .10 level of significance $t_c = 1.658$.

a.   **DEF and RPRR**:

$r = .5105786$
$$t_m = \frac{.5105786\sqrt{72 - 2}}{\sqrt{1 - .51057862}} = 4.968$$

Since 4.968 is greater than 1.980, H_0 is rejected at a 0.05 level of significance. It is appropriate to conclude, therefore, that significant positive correlation exists.

b.   **TDEF and RPRR**: $r = .40$; $t_m = 3.61 > 1.980$.
H_0 is rejected. It is concluded that significant positive autocorrelation exists.

c.   **DEF and MNS**: $r = .81$; $t_m = 12.05 > 1.980$.
H_0 is rejected. It is concluded that significant positive correlation exists.

4.1 Exercises

Questions for Review:

4.1-1.   General functional form: $NTO_t = f(RGNP_t)$

Specific functional form: $NTO_t = b_0 + b_1(RGNP_t)$

4.1-2.   The correlation coefficient, $r_{NTO \cdot RGNP}$ measures the relative degree of the linear relationship between NTO and RGNP. The general functional form presented in Exercise 4.1-1, however, suggests a causal relationship where $RGNP_t$ has an explanatory impact on NTO_t. In the specific functional form of Exercise 4.1-1, the explanatory relationship between NTO and RGNP is specified as a linear one.

4.1-3.   For example,

Quantity = f(Price)

Total product = f(Labor input holding capital constant)

Bond price = f(Interest rate)

4.1-4.   For example,

Sales = f(Advertising expenditures)

Risk of cancer = f(Cigarette smoking)

Exam scores = f(IQ level)

Exam scores = f(Hours studied)

4.1-5.   A normative-based statement involves a value judgment such as "Inflation creates misery." A positive-based approach, however, involves an objective explanation based on some causal relationship. An example of a positive argument is, "Inflation is caused by rapid growth in the money supply."

4.1-6.   It provides the tools to test theoretical relationships thereby helping scientists to choose between competing theories. By making it possible to measure theoretical relationships more accurately, econometrics facilitates the forecasting process and normative policy evaluation.

4.1-7.   If $b_1 = 0.95$, the government spending multiplier is 20 instead of 10 in the case where b_1 is assumed to be equal to 0.9.

33

$$\frac{\partial Y_t}{\partial G_t} = \frac{1}{1 - 0.95} = \frac{1}{0.05} = 20 \qquad \text{See equation (4.1-11)}$$

This result suggests that a $10 billion increase in government spending will result in a twenty-fold increase in aggregate income ($200 billion) rather than the ten-fold increase ($100 billion) estimated in the text when b_1 is assumed to be 0.9.

Similarly, if $b_1 = 0.95$, the tax multiplier is -19 instead of -9 obtained when b_1 is assumed to be 0.9:

$$\frac{\partial Y_t}{\partial T_t} = \frac{-b_1}{1 - b_1} = \frac{-0.95}{1 - 0.95} = \frac{-0.95}{0.05} = -19 \quad \text{See equation (4.1-12)}$$

This result suggests that a $10 billion increase in taxes will result in a nineteen-fold decrease in aggregate income (-$190 billion) rather than the nine-fold decrease (-$90 billion) estimated in the text when b_1 is assumed to be 0.9.

Hence, a small change in the assumed value of the marginal propensity to consume (b_1) has a significant effect on the estimated impact of fiscal policy.

4.1-8. *Specification* refers to the selection of variables to be included in an equation as well as the functional form of the relationship.

4.2 Exercises

Questions for Review:

4.2-1. Since perfectly linear relationships rarely exist between economic and social variables, error terms (e_t) will likely be some non-zero value, the assumption in (4.2-6) suggests that the best "guess" about e_t is that it will be equal to zero. This assumption suggests that the average value of all the error terms over time (t) is also equal to zero. The assumption in (4.2-7) implies that the dispersion or spread of the error term away from zero (i.e., $\mu_e = 0$) is constant over time. Assumptions (4.2-8) and (4.2-9) suggest that no measurable relationship exists between any of the error terms or between the error terms and the independent variable, respectively.

4.2-2. b_1 is the actual parameter or coefficient obtained when a regression equation is estimated using a population of x and y data. $\hat{b}_1$, on the other hand, is the estimated parameter obtained when a sample (subset of the population) of the data is used.

4.2-3. The forecasting process is facilitated when lagged values are used in regression equations since actual values of the independent variable can be used to forecast future values of the dependent variable.

4.2-4. Solving for $\hat{b}_0$ and $\hat{b}_1$ over the 1965:1 to 1966:4 sample period:

OBS.	$NTOl_t$	$RGNP_t$	$(NTOl_t)(RGNP_t)$	$RGNP_t^2$
1965:1	2,600.3	906.6	2,357,431.98	821,923.56
1965:2	2,681.4	919.6	2,465,815.44	845,664.16
1965:3	2,728.1	934.0	2,548,045.40	872,356.00
1965:4	2,781.9	956.8	2,661,721.92	915,466.24
1966:1	2,738.9	975.4	2,671,327.98	951,405.16
1966:2	2,820.3	979.4	2,762,201.82	959,224.36
1966:3	2,870.7	987.9	2,835,964.53	975,946.41
1966:4	2,922.7	996.7	2,913,055.09	993,410.89
Total			21,215,564.16	7,335,396.78

$$\hat{b}_1 = \frac{21,215,564.16 - 8(957)(2768)}{7,335,396.78 - 8(957)^2} = \frac{23,756.16}{8,604.78} = 2.76$$

$$\hat{b}_0 = 2,768 - 2.76(957) = 126.68$$

$$y_t = 126.68 + 2.76x_t + e_t \text{ or } \hat{y}_t = 126.68 + 2.76\ x_t$$

$$\widehat{NTOl}_t = 126.68 + 2.76\ RGNP_t$$

For Orange County the estimated equation is:

$$\widehat{NTO}_t = -197.0 + 0.535 RGNP_t.$$

There is a positive relationship between RGNP and total wage and salary employment in both areas. However, a one unit increase in RGNP creates 2.76 jobs in Chicago compared to about 0.54 jobs in Orange County.

Computer Exercises:

4.2-5.   >*FETCH GNP PDE NTO NTO1*
            >*GENR RGNP=GNP/PDE*
            >*SMPL 65.1 66.4*
            >*LS NTO1 C RGNP*

```
SMPL   1965.1 - 1966.4
8 Observations
LS // Dependent Variable is NTO1
===================================================================
       VARIABLE    COEFFICIENT   STD. ERROR    T-STAT.   2-TAIL SIG.
===================================================================
          C         14486.618    455047.01    0.0318354   0.976
          RGNP      2877.1088     475.21626    6.0543147   0.001
===================================================================
R-squared               0.859336   Mean of dependent var   2768013.
Adjusted R-squared      0.835892   S.D. of dependent var   103841.4
S.E. of regression      42066.45   Sum of squared resid    1.06D+10
Durbin-Watson stat      1.675022   F-statistic             36.65473
Log likelihood         -95.37683
===================================================================
                        Covariance Matrix
===================================================================
C,C                     2.07D+11   C,RGNP                 -2.16D+08
RGNP,RGNP               225830.5
===================================================================


===================================================================
         Residual Plot              obs RESIDUAL  ACTUAL   FITTED
===================================================================
|        :    *   |         :     | 65.1 -22578.1 2600300  2622878
|        :        |   *     :     | 65.2  21122.1 2681400  2660278
|        :        |    *    :     | 65.3  26356.8 2728100  2701743
|        :        |   *     :     | 65.4  14662.0 2781900  2767238
|   *    :        |         :     | 66.1 -82212.3 2738700  2820912
|        :     *  |         :     | 66.2 -11934.8 2820300  2832235
|        :        |   *     :     | 66.3  13858.7 2870700  2856841
|        :        |       *:      | 66.4  40725.7 2922700  2881974
===================================================================
```

> *SMPL 65.1 83.4*
> *LS NTO1 C RGNP*

```
SMPL   1965.1 - 1983.4
76 Observations
LS // Dependent Variable is NTO1
===================================================================
       VARIABLE    COEFFICIENT   STD. ERROR    T-STAT.   2-TAIL SIG.
===================================================================
          C         2268395.0    52202.229    43.453988   0.000
          RGNP      606.71717     41.201458    14.725624   0.000
===================================================================
R-squared               0.745568   Mean of dependent var   3028143.
```

Adjusted R-squared	0.742130	S.D. of dependent var	136446.3
S.E. of regression	69288.67	Sum of squared resid	3.55D+11
Durbin-Watson stat	0.498309	F-statistic	216.8440
Log likelihood	-953.9247		

===
Covariance Matrix
===

C,C	2.73D+09	C,RGNP	-2125733.
RGNP,RGNP	1697.560		

===

===

Residual Plot	obs	RESIDUAL	ACTUAL	FITTED
===
| * : | :	65.1	-218146.	2600300	2818446
| * : | :	65.2	-144933.	2681400	2826333
| * : | :	65.3	-106977.	2728100	2835077
| * | :	65.4	-66988.1	2781900	2848888
| * : | :	66.1	-121507.	2738700	2860207
| : * | :	66.2	-42294.4	2820300	2862594
| : * :	66.3	2916.65	2870700	2867783
| : | * :	66.4	49616.7	2922700	2873083
| : * | :	67.1	-22316.6	2851400	2873717
| : |* :	67.2	22038.4	2899700	2877662
| : | *:	67.3	61515.9	2946500	2884984
| : | *	67.4	70930.4	2962700	2891770
| : |* :	68.1	8582.55	2905900	2897317
| : | *:	68.2	53257.8	2962200	2908942
| : | *	68.3	73107.3	2989600	2916493
| : | : *	68.4	98457.0	3017200	2918743
| : | * :	69.1	40434.4	2966600	2926166
| : | : *	69.2	95951.4	3024900	2928949
| : | : *	69.3	127033.	3057900	2930867
| : | : *	69.4	130793.	3057800	2927007
| : | *:	70.1	57448.3	2981900	2924452
| : | *:	70.2	51022.4	2976500	2925478
| : | *	70.3	73241.7	3005000	2931758
| : | *:	70.4	60662.0	2987100	2926438
| : * | :	71.1	-43789.7	2899000	2942790
| : * : :	71.2	-154.416	2945900	2946054
| : |* :	71.3	17576.7	2969000	2951423
| : * : :	71.4	5217.02	2962500	2957283
| * | :	72.1	-70795.4	2899700	2970495
| : * | :	72.2	-23033.1	2960400	2983433
| : * : :	72.3	-1579.57	2990700	2992280
| : *| :	72.4	-11530.2	2993900	3005430
| * | :	73.1	-71302.7	2953500	3024803

37

```
|          :    |*    :   | 73.2   15636.9   3041400   3025763
|          :    | *   :   | 73.3   50848.4   3081100   3030252
|          :    |    *    | 73.4   72472.5   3109000   3036527
|          :    | *   :   | 74.1   27880.8   3056700   3028819
|          :    |    *    | 74.2   79874.5   3109500   3029625
|          :    |    :  * | 74.3   101211.   3126100   3024889
|          :    |    :  * | 74.4   102749.   3117600   3014851
|          :   *|    :    | 75.1  -17642.7   2981400   2999043
|          : *  |    :    | 75.2  -37374.0   2970500   3007874
|          :*   |    :    | 75.3  -51396.8   2973000   3024397
|          : *  |    :    | 75.4  -43524.8   2987700   3031225
|      *   :    |    :    | 76.1  -116107.   2931900   3048007
|          :*   |    :    | 76.2  -65392.3   2987900   3053292
|          :   *|    :    | 76.3  -8780.21   3049000   3057780
|          :   *|    :    | 76.4  -19326.6   3045500   3064827
|      *   :    |    :    | 77.1  -121641.   2960500   3082141
|          : *  |    :    | 77.2  -31922.2   3063600   3095522
|          : *  |    :    | 77.3  -26786.1   3082400   3109186
|          :    *    :    | 77.4   4672.70   3115500   3110827
|          :*   |    :    | 78.1  -54707.6   3063100   3117808
|          :   *|    :    | 78.2  -10727.6   3129500   3140228
|          :    | *  :    | 78.3   33779.2   3181200   3147421
|          :    | *  :    | 78.4   24501.5   3183800   3159299
|          :   *|    :    | 79.1  -18530.4   3143300   3161830
|          :    | *:      | 79.2   52616.1   3212400   3159784
|          :    |    *    | 79.3   71513.1   3241900   3170387
|          :    |    :*   | 79.4   85773.7   3257800   3172026
|          :    |*   :    | 80.1   19217.0   3195500   3176283
|          :    |    *    | 80.2   73743.7   3228800   3155056
|          :    |    *    | 80.3   77041.2   3233800   3156759
|          :    |    *:   | 80.4   58549.8   3223600   3165050
|          :   *|    :    | 81.1  -14691.4   3169900   3184591
|          :    *    :    | 81.2   6335.54   3192400   3186064
|          :   *|    :    | 81.3  -12021.1   3182100   3194121
|          :   *|    :    | 81.4  -12962.0   3169700   3182662
|         *     |    :    | 82.1  -75319.0   3094500   3169819
|         *     |    :    | 82.2  -74181.3   3097800   3171981
|        *:     |    :    | 82.3  -84394.1   3085400   3169794
|       *  :    |    :    | 82.4  -122699.   3044100   3166799
|          :*   |    :    | 83.1  -62198.3   3110300   3172498
|          : *  |    :    | 83.2  -38070.3   3155600   3193670
|          :    *    :    | 83.3   2124.43   3213000   3210876
|          :    *    :    | 83.4   5398.97   3227500   3222101
=============================================================================
```

>*SMPL 65.1 66.4*
>*LS NTO C RGNP*

```
SMPL  1965.1 - 1966.4
8 Observations
LS // Dependent Variable is NTO
=================================================================
        VARIABLE    COEFFICIENT   STD. ERROR    T-STAT.   2-TAIL SIG.
=================================================================
            C       -207970.38    73028.372   -2.8478025   0.029
          RGNP       546.48789     76.265241    7.1656220   0.000
=================================================================
R-squared                0.895372   Mean of dependent var    315043.8
Adjusted R-squared       0.877934   S.D. of dependent var    19322.99
S.E. of regression       6751.049   Sum of squared resid     2.73D+08
Durbin-Watson stat       1.425263   F-statistic              51.34614
Log likelihood          -80.74041
=================================================================
                         Covariance Matrix
=================================================================
C,C                     5.33D+09   C,RGNP                   -5566551.
RGNP,RGNP               5816.387
=================================================================


=================================================================
          Residual Plot               obs RESIDUAL  ACTUAL   FITTED
=================================================================
|        :    |*    :    |  65.1   523.577  288000.  287476.
|        :    |    *  :   |  65.2  4169.73   298750.  294580.
|        :    |  *    :   |  65.3   323.658  302780.  302456.
|        *    |       :   |  65.4 -6246.65   308650.  314897.
|   *    :    |       :   |  66.1 -12361.7   312730.  325092.
|        :    |    *  :   |  66.2  4207.64   331450.  327242.
|        :    |     *:    |  66.3  5723.81   337640.  331916.
|        :    |   *   :   |  66.4  3659.95   340350.  336690.
=================================================================
```

>*SMPL 65.1 83.4*
>*LS NTO C RGNP*

```
SMPL  1965.1 - 1983.4
76 Observations
LS // Dependent Variable is NTO
=================================================================
        VARIABLE    COEFFICIENT   STD. ERROR    T-STAT.   2-TAIL SIG.
=================================================================
            C       -672969.88    20216.061   -33.288872   0.000
          RGNP       1003.7824     15.955855    62.909972   0.000
=================================================================
R-squared                0.981645   Mean of dependent var    583994.8
```

39

```
Adjusted R-squared        0.981397    S.D. of dependent var    196734.8
S.E. of regression        26833.03    Sum of squared resid     5.33D+10
Durbin-Watson stat        0.302290    F-statistic              3957.665
Log likelihood            -881.8275
====================================================================
                          Covariance Matrix
====================================================================
C,C                       4.09D+08    C,RGNP                  -318803.9
RGNP,RGNP                 254.5893
====================================================================
```

```
====================================================================
          Residual Plot                  obs RESIDUAL  ACTUAL   FITTED
====================================================================
|         :        |     :     *  |  65.1  50939.1  288000.  237061.
|         :        |     :     *  |  65.2  48640.9  298750.  250109.
|         :        |     :  *     |  65.3  38204.2  302780.  264576.
|         :        |   *:         |  65.4  21224.0  308650.  287426.
|         :        |*   :         |  66.1  6577.78  312730.  306152.
|         :        |  *:          |  66.2  21347.5  331450.  310102.
|         :        |  *  :        |  66.3  18952.7  337640.  318687.
|         :        | *   :        |  66.4  12894.1  340350.  327456.
|         :        | *   :        |  67.1  10256.5  338760.  328504.
|         :        |   *:         |  67.2  22099.6  357130.  335030.
|         :        |  *  :        |  67.3  17154.9  364300.  347145.
|         :        | *   :        |  67.4  13258.7  371630.  358371.
|         :        |*    :        |  68.1  3880.04  371430.  367550.
|         :      * |     :        |  68.2 -1952.46  384830.  386782.
|         :   *    |     :        |  68.3 -9214.48  390060.  399274.
|         :     *| |     :        |  68.4 -6770.49  396227.  402997.
|         :  *     |     :        |  69.1 -18917.8  396360.  415278.
|         :     *| |     :        |  69.2 -4842.16  415040.  419882.
|         :     *| |     :        |  69.3 -4856.11  418200.  423056.
|         :        |*    :        |  69.4  6019.89  422690.  416670.
|         :        | *   :        |  70.1  10927.9  423370.  412442.
|         :        |  *  :        |  70.2  17730.5  431870.  414139.
|         :      * |     :        |  70.3  979.341  425510.  424531.
|         :        |*    :        |  70.4  4571.55  420300.  415728.
|         *        |     :        |  71.1 -25681.4  417100.  442781.
|         :   *    |     :        |  71.2 -14352.8  433830.  448183.
|         :   *    |     :        |  71.3 -17775.2  439290.  457065.
|         :*       |     :        |  71.4 -24289.9  442470.  466760.
|         *:       |     :        |  72.1 -29909.2  458710.  488619.
|         *        |     :        |  72.2 -29123.8  480900.  510024.
|       * :        |     :        |  72.3 -39449.9  485210.  524660.
|     *   :        |     :        |  72.4 -50586.9  495830.  546417.
| *       :        |     :        |  73.1 -68751.8  509716.  578468.
```

```
|      *  :    |    :        | 73.2 -41886.8  538170.  580057.
|     *   :    |    :        | 73.3 -45112.7  542370.  587483.
|    *    :    |    :        | 73.4 -49745.8  548120.  597866.
|     * : :    |    :        | 74.1 -38052.8  547060.  585113.
|       : *  | |    :        | 74.2 -14456.8  571990.  586447.
|       :  * | |    :        | 74.3 -6931.26  571680.  578611.
|       :    | *  :          | 74.4  11626.4  573630.  562004.
|       :    | *  :          | 75.1  14570.8  550420.  535849.
|       :    |  * :          | 75.2  16199.9  566660.  550460.
|       :  *|    :           | 75.3 -6276.17  571520.  577796.
|       :  *|    :           | 75.4 -2422.77  586670.  589093.
|       *   |    :           | 76.1 -26658.4  590200.  616858.
|       :  * |   :           | 76.2 -9812.29  615790.  625602.
|      : *  |    :           | 76.3 -18297.4  614730.  633027.
|       :  *|    :           | 76.4 -4915.19  639770.  644685.
|       *   |    :           | 77.1 -26201.2  647130.  673331.
|       :  * |   :           | 77.2 -14899.6  680570.  695470.
|      *:   |    :           | 77.3 -31695.7  686380.  718076.
|       :  * |   :           | 77.4 -10131.1  710660.  720791.
|       :  * |   :           | 78.1 -10209.6  722130.  732340.
|       :  * |   :           | 78.2 -12539.4  756893.  769432.
|       :*  |    :           | 78.3 -21126.2  760207.  781333.
|       : * |    :           | 78.4 -17258.2  783726.  800984.
|       :*  |    :           | 79.1 -20873.0  784300.  805173.
|       :  *|    :           | 79.2 -2457.18  799330.  801787.
|       : * |    :           | 79.3 -7593.36  811736.  819329.
|       :    | *  :          | 79.4  16855.4  838897.  822042.
|       :    |*   :          | 80.1  2382.87  831467.  829084.
|       :    |    :    *      | 80.2  50404.3  844370.  793966.
|       :    |    :   *       | 80.3  41150.6  837933.  796782.
|       :    |    :   *       | 80.4  46636.9  857137.  810500.
|       :    | *  :          | 81.1  17303.1  860133.  842830.
|       :    |    :*         | 81.2  31659.9  876927.  845267.
|       :    | *  :          | 81.3  14134.7  872731.  858596.
|       :    |    : *        | 81.4  37658.2  877296.  839638.
|       :    |    :  *        | 82.1  43012.2  861402.  818390.
|       :    |    :  *        | 82.2  44092.8  866060.  821967.
|       :    |   *            | 82.3  28377.4  846726.  818349.
|       :    |    : *        | 82.4  38234.1  851627.  813393.
|       :    |   *            | 83.1  28507.5  851330.  822823.
|       :    | *  :          | 83.2  17574.5  875425.  857850.
|       : *  |    :           | 83.3 -18257.8  868058.  886316.
|       :*   |    :           | 83.4 -21755.7  883132.  904888.
```

As expected, the coefficient of RGNP in all four regression equations is positive, indicating a positive relationship between real GNP and employment levels in both Chicago and Orange County.

During the 1965 to 1983 period, the coefficient of RGNP is 607.7 for Chicago and 1003.8 for Orange County. Hence, the estimated equations suggest that a one unit increase in real GNP will create 1003.7 jobs in Orange County versus 607.7 jobs in Chicago.

4.2-6. The estimated regression equation is the equation of the line which best fits the actual data. Since some of the actual data will always lie below or above the best fitted line, residuals will always occur.

From the residual plots shown in Exercise 4.2-6, the five highest residuals for the estimated equations over 1965:1 to 1966:4 are as follows:

Chicago		Orange County	
1965:2	21,122.1	1965:2	4,169.73
1965:3	26,356.8	1965:4	-6,246.65
1965:4	14,662.0	1966:1	-12,361.70
1966:1	-82,212.3	1966:2	4,207.64
1966:4	40,725.7	1966:3	5,723.81

The five highest residuals for the estimated equations over 1965:1 to 1983:4 are:

Chicago		Orange County	
1965:1	-218,146	1965:1	50,939.1
1965:2	-144,933	1972:4	-50,586.9
1969:3	127,033	1973:1	-68,751.8
1969:4	130,793	1973:4	-49,745.8
1982:4	-122,699	1980:2	50,404.3

4.2-7.
>*FETCH GNP PDE NMI1 NCN1 NMN1 NTR1 NWR1 NFI1 NSR1 NGV1*
>*GENR RGNP=GNP/PDE*
>*LS NMI1 C RGNP*

SMPL   1965.1 - 1983.4
76 Observations
LS // Dependent Variable is NMI1
===
       VARIABLE   COEFFICIENT   STD. ERROR   T-STAT.   2-TAIL SIG.
===
          C   8978.7964   473.55490   18.960413   0.000
         RGNP   -3.3880076   0.3737609   -9.0646386   0.000
===
R-squared   0.526150   Mean of dependent var   4736.238
Adjusted R-squared   0.519747   S.D. of dependent var   907.0024
S.E. of regression   628.5553   Sum of squared resid   29236054
Durbin-Watson stat   0.242828   F-statistic   82.16767
Log likelihood   -596.5262
===

>*LS NCN1 C RGNP*

SMPL   1965.1 - 1983.4
76 Observations
LS // Dependent Variable is NCN1
===
       VARIABLE   COEFFICIENT   STD. ERROR   T-STAT.   2-TAIL SIG.
===
          C   129123.62   9613.7346   13.431161   0.000
         RGNP   -11.836941   7.5877964   -1.5599972   0.123
===
R-squared   0.031839   Mean of dependent var   114301.1
Adjusted R-squared   0.018756   S.D. of dependent var   12881.81
S.E. of regression   12760.43   Sum of squared resid   1.20D+10
Durbin-Watson stat   1.038134   F-statistic   2.433591
Log likelihood   -825.3379
===

43

>*LS NMN1 C RGNP*

```
SMPL   1965.1 - 1983.4
76 Observations
LS // Dependent Variable is NMN1
========================================================================
      VARIABLE    COEFFICIENT   STD. ERROR    T-STAT.   2-TAIL SIG.
========================================================================
         C         1351731.4    37899.671    35.666045    0.000
         RGNP     -387.26460    29.912931   -12.946394    0.000
========================================================================
R-squared              0.693720   Mean of dependent var     866787.7
Adjusted R-squared     0.689581   S.D. of dependent var     90288.96
S.E. of regression     50304.71   Sum of squared resid      1.87D+11
Durbin-Watson stat     0.146123   F-statistic               167.6091
Log likelihood        -929.5908
========================================================================
```

>*LS NTR1 C RGNP*

```
SMPL   1965.1 - 1983.4
76 Observations
LS // Dependent Variable is NTR1
========================================================================
      VARIABLE    COEFFICIENT   STD. ERROR    T-STAT.   2-TAIL SIG.
========================================================================
         C         226604.10    4636.8828    48.869921    0.000
         RGNP     -23.156121    3.6597352    -6.3272668   0.000
========================================================================
R-squared              0.351072   Mean of dependent var     197607.3
Adjusted R-squared     0.342303   S.D. of dependent var     7589.033
S.E. of regression     6154.592   Sum of squared resid      2.80D+09
Durbin-Watson stat     0.723118   F-statistic               40.03431
Log likelihood        -769.9224
========================================================================
```

>*LS NWR1 C RGNP*

```
SMPL  1965.1 - 1983.4
76 Observations
LS // Dependent Variable is NWR1
```

===

VARIABLE	COEFFICIENT	STD. ERROR	T-STAT.	2-TAIL SIG.

===

| C | 353290.62 | 12163.793 | 29.044447 | 0.000 |
| RGNP | 270.97788 | 9.6004711 | 28.225478 | 0.000 |

===

R-squared	0.915009	Mean of dependent var	692616.8
Adjusted R-squared	0.913860	S.D. of dependent var	55009.82
S.E. of regression	16145.15	Sum of squared resid	1.93D+10
Durbin-Watson stat	1.232377	F-statistic	796.6776
Log likelihood	-843.2184		

===

>*LS NFI1 C RGNP*

```
SMPL  1965.1 - 1983.4
76 Observations
LS // Dependent Variable is NFI1
```

===

VARIABLE	COEFFICIENT	STD. ERROR	T-STAT.	2-TAIL SIG.

===

| C | 27785.479 | 6378.8324 | 4.3558879 | 0.000 |
| RGNP | 136.01373 | 5.0345973 | 27.015812 | 0.000 |

===

R-squared	0.907943	Mean of dependent var	198105.7
Adjusted R-squared	0.906699	S.D. of dependent var	27718.67
S.E. of regression	8466.704	Sum of squared resid	5.30D+09
Durbin-Watson stat	0.186750	F-statistic	729.8541
Log likelihood	-794.1621		

===

45

>*LS NSR1 C RGNP*

```
SMPL   1965.1 - 1983.4
76 Observations
LS // Dependent Variable is NSR1
======================================================================
        VARIABLE   COEFFICIENT   STD. ERROR     T-STAT.   2-TAIL SIG.
======================================================================
           C        16165.034    18761.246     0.8616184     0.392
        RGNP        445.09895    14.807618     30.058780     0.000
======================================================================
R-squared                0.924299   Mean of dependent var   573530.5
Adjusted R-squared       0.923276   S.D. of dependent var   89901.99
S.E. of regression       24902.04   Sum of squared resid    4.59D+10
Durbin-Watson stat       0.199573   F-statistic             903.5303
Log likelihood           -876.1515
======================================================================
```

>*LS NGV1 C RGNP*

```
SMPL   1965.1 - 1983.4
76 Observations
LS // Dependent Variable is NGV1
======================================================================
        VARIABLE   COEFFICIENT   STD. ERROR     T-STAT.   2-TAIL SIG.
======================================================================
           C        154716.00    15185.159    10.188632     0.000
        RGNP        180.27231    11.985134    15.041326     0.000
======================================================================
R-squared                0.753532   Mean of dependent var   380458.1
Adjusted R-squared       0.750201   S.D. of dependent var   40327.12
S.E. of regression       20155.45   Sum of squared resid    3.01D+10
Durbin-Watson stat       0.110162   F-statistic             226.2415
Log likelihood           -860.0794
======================================================================
```

46

>*LS NTO1 C RGNP*

SMPL 1965.1 - 1983.4
76 Observations
LS // Dependent Variable is NTO1
==
        VARIABLE   COEFFICIENT   STD. ERROR   T-STAT.   2-TAIL SIG.
==
           C   2268395.0   52202.229   43.453988   0.000
        RGNP   606.71717   41.201458   14.725624   0.000
==
R-squared   0.745568   Mean of dependent var   3028143.
Adjusted R-squared   0.742130   S.D. of dependent var   136446.3
S.E. of regression   69288.67   Sum of squared resid   3.55D+11
Durbin-Watson stat   0.498309   F-statistic   216.8440
Log likelihood   -953.9247
==

4.2-8.   >*FETCH GNP PDE NMI1 NCN1 NMN1 NTR1 NWR1 NFI1 NSR1 NGV1*
          >*GENR RGNP=GNP/PDE*
          >*SMPL 65.2 83.4*
          >*LS NMI1 C RGNP(-1)*

SMPL 1965.2 - 1983.4
75 Observations
LS // Dependent Variable is NMI1
==
        VARIABLE   COEFFICIENT   STD. ERROR   T-STAT.   2-TAIL SIG.
==
           C   8893.3216   482.14891   18.445176   0.000
        RGNP(-1)   -3.3467270   0.3819193   -8.7629168   0.000
==
R-squared   0.512647   Mean of dependent var   4716.721
Adjusted R-squared   0.505971   S.D. of dependent var   896.9004
S.E. of regression   630.4063   Sum of squared resid   29011079
Durbin-Watson stat   0.255277   F-statistic   76.78871
Log likelihood   -588.8841
==

47

>*LS NCN1 C RGNP(-1)*

```
SMPL   1965.2 - 1983.4
75 Observations
LS // Dependent Variable is NCN1
==================================================================
      VARIABLE    COEFFICIENT   STD. ERROR    T-STAT.   2-TAIL SIG.
==================================================================
         C        133294.31    9493.3302    14.040838    0.000
      RGNP(-1)    -14.961866    7.5198469    -1.9896503   0.051
==================================================================
R-squared               0.051439    Mean of dependent var   114622.4
Adjusted R-squared      0.038445    S.D. of dependent var   12658.17
S.E. of regression      12412.46    Sum of squared resid    1.12D+10
Durbin-Watson stat      1.088932    F-statistic             3.958708
Log likelihood         -812.3910
==================================================================
```

>*LS NMN1 C RGNP(-1)*

```
SMPL   1965.2 - 1983.4
75 Observations
LS // Dependent Variable is NMN1
==================================================================
      VARIABLE    COEFFICIENT   STD. ERROR    T-STAT.   2-TAIL SIG.
==================================================================
         C        1361332.6    38195.335    35.641330    0.000
      RGNP(-1)    -396.58543    30.255250   -13.107987    0.000
==================================================================
R-squared               0.701821    Mean of dependent var   866407.5
Adjusted R-squared      0.697736    S.D. of dependent var   90835.72
S.E. of regression      49940.13    Sum of squared resid    1.82D+11
Durbin-Watson stat      0.155683    F-statistic             171.8193
Log likelihood         -916.8003
==================================================================
```

>*LS NTR1 C RGNP(-1)*

SMPL   1965.2 - 1983.4
75 Observations
LS // Dependent Variable is NTR1
===
VARIABLE	COEFFICIENT	STD. ERROR	T-STAT.	2-TAIL SIG.
C	228080.44	4624.6404	49.318525	0.000
RGNP(-1)	-24.356168	3.6632654	-6.6487590	0.000
===
R-squared	0.377165	Mean of dependent var	197684.8
Adjusted R-squared	0.368633	S.D. of dependent var	7609.854
S.E. of regression	6046.684	Sum of squared resid	2.67D+09
Durbin-Watson stat	0.763805	F-statistic	44.20600
Log likelihood	-758.4517		
===

>*LS NWR1 C RGNP(-1)*

SMPL   1965.2 - 1983.4
75 Observations
LS // Dependent Variable is NWR1
===
VARIABLE	COEFFICIENT	STD. ERROR	T-STAT.	2-TAIL SIG.
C	360863.54	11060.892	32.625176	0.000
RGNP(-1)	267.22431	8.7615422	30.499688	0.000
===
R-squared	0.927235	Mean of dependent var	694350.3
Adjusted R-squared	0.926238	S.D. of dependent var	53249.32
S.E. of regression	14462.04	Sum of squared resid	1.53D+10
Durbin-Watson stat	1.360934	F-statistic	930.2310
Log likelihood	-823.8530		
===

>*LS NFI1 C RGNP(-1)*

```
SMPL   1965.2 - 1983.4
75 Observations
LS // Dependent Variable is NFI1
===================================================================
    VARIABLE    COEFFICIENT   STD. ERROR    T-STAT.    2-TAIL SIG.
===================================================================
       C         28448.808    6382.3465    4.4574213     0.000
     RGNP(-1)    136.40303    5.0555777    26.980701      0.000
===================================================================
R-squared              0.908859    Mean of dependent var    198675.1
Adjusted R-squared     0.907611    S.D. of dependent var    27454.20
S.E. of regression     8344.872    Sum of squared resid     5.08D+09
Durbin-Watson stat     0.196104    F-statistic              727.9582
Log likelihood         -782.6120
===================================================================
```

>*LS NSR1 C RGNP(-1)*

```
SMPL   1965.2 - 1983.4
75 Observations
LS // Dependent Variable is NSR1
===================================================================
    VARIABLE    COEFFICIENT   STD. ERROR    T-STAT.    2-TAIL SIG.
===================================================================
       C         20849.991    18666.479    1.1169751     0.268
     RGNP(-1)    444.52040    14.786072    30.063455      0.000
===================================================================
R-squared              0.925267    Mean of dependent var    575596.3
Adjusted R-squared     0.924243    S.D. of dependent var    88672.96
S.E. of regression     24406.29    Sum of squared resid     4.35D+10
Durbin-Watson stat     0.187760    F-statistic              903.8113
Log likelihood         -863.1015
===================================================================
```

>*LS NGV1 C RGNP(-1)*

```
SMPL  1965.2 - 1983.4
75 Observations
LS // Dependent Variable is NGV1
========================================================================
      VARIABLE   COEFFICIENT   STD. ERROR     T-STAT.   2-TAIL SIG.
========================================================================
         C        164019.74    15195.902    10.793682     0.000
      RGNP(-1)    174.50407    12.036962    14.497351     0.000
========================================================================
R-squared             0.742207   Mean of dependent var   381794.9
Adjusted R-squared    0.738676   S.D. of dependent var   38866.55
S.E. of regression    19868.53   Sum of squared resid    2.88D+10
Durbin-Watson stat    0.117481   F-statistic             210.1732
Log likelihood       -847.6738
========================================================================
```

>*LS NTO1 C RGNP(-1)*

```
SMPL  1965.2 - 1983.4
75 Observations
LS // Dependent Variable is NTO1
========================================================================
      VARIABLE   COEFFICIENT   STD. ERROR     T-STAT.   2-TAIL SIG.
========================================================================
         C        2305782.7    47662.445    48.377349     0.000
      RGNP(-1)    583.40160    37.754326    15.452576     0.000
========================================================================
R-squared             0.765862   Mean of dependent var   3033848.
Adjusted R-squared    0.762655   S.D. of dependent var   127916.1
S.E. of regression    62318.31   Sum of squared resid    2.84D+11
Durbin-Watson stat    0.563561   F-statistic             238.7821
Log likelihood       -933.4076
========================================================================
```

Study Project:

4.2-9. $SSQ = \Sigma(y_t - \hat{y}_t)^2 = (y_t - \hat{b}_0 - \hat{b}_1 x_t)^2$

$$\frac{\partial SSQ}{\partial \hat{b}_0} = 2(y_t - \hat{b}_0 - \hat{b}_1 x_t)(-1) = 0$$

$$\frac{\partial SSQ}{\partial \hat{b}_1} = 2(y_t - \hat{b}_0 - \hat{b}_1 x_t)(-x_t) = 0$$

51

Simplifying the above:

$$\Sigma y_t = n\hat{b}_0 + \hat{b}_1 \Sigma x_t \text{ or } \bar{y} = \hat{b}_0 + \hat{b}_1 \bar{x} \text{ and}$$

$$\Sigma(y_t x_t) = \hat{b}_0 \Sigma x_t + \hat{b}_1 \Sigma x_t^2$$

The above equations are the same as equations (4.2-13) and (4.2-16) as shown in the text after dividing equation (4.2-16) by n.

4.3 Exercises

Questions for Review:

4.3-1.   Unexplained variation $= e_t = NTO_t - \widehat{NTO}_t$

OBS.	NTO_t	$\widehat{NTO}_t$	$(NTO_t - \widehat{NTO}_t)$	$(NTO_t - \overline{NTO})^2$
1965:1	288.0	287.5	0.25	729.00
1965:2	298.7	294.6	16.81	265.69
1965:3	302.7	302.5	0.04	151.29
1965:4	308.7	314.9	38.44	39.69
1966:1	312.7	325.1	153.76	5.29
1966:2	331.5	327.3	17.64	272.25
1966:3	337.6	331.9	32.49	510.76
1966:4	340.3	336.7	12.96	640.09
Total	2,520.2		272.39	2,614.06

$$R^2 = 1 - \frac{\Sigma(NTO_t - \widehat{NTO}_t)^2}{\Sigma(NTO_t - \overline{NTO})^2} = 1 - \frac{272.39}{2,614.06} = 1 - 0.10 = 0.89$$

Notice that the above result is the same as the R^2 value derived in Table 4.3-1 shown in the text.

4.3-2.   The R^2 value is a measure of association and does not test for the direction of causation between two variables. Hence, a high R^2 value may simply measure the common trend between two unrelated variables. In addition, a high R^2 value is more likely to occur when measuring the association between stable rather than erratic series. Yet, an equation with a low R^2 that explains the association between two erratic series may be a more useful explanatory tool than an equation with a high R^2 value that measures the association between two stable series.

4.3-3. $\widehat{NTO}_t = -670,591.1 + 1,008.5(1,248) = 588,016.8$

$$S_{ef} = 24,316 \sqrt{1 + \frac{1}{75} + \frac{1,248 - 1,248}{2,724,658}} = 24,478$$

At a 0.05 level of significance, the appropriate confidence interval is

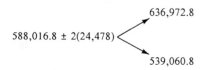

$$588,016.8 \pm 2(24,478) \underset{539,060.8}{\overset{636,972.8}{\diagup}}$$

The interval of 539,060.8 to 636,972.8 compares to a wider interval of 864,774 to 964,566 (See figure 4.5-5) when the $RGNP_{83:4}$ level of 1,571.9 is used.

4.3-4.

$$H_0: b_1 = 0$$
$$H_1: b_1 \neq 0$$

$$F_m = \frac{\Sigma(\hat{y}_t - \bar{y})^2/1}{\Sigma(y_t - \hat{y})^2/n - 2}$$

With one degree of freedom for the numerator and 74 degrees of freedom (n - 2) for the denominator, $F_c{}^{.05} = 4.00$ and $F_c{}^{.01} = 7.08$.

From exercise 4.2-7 the measured F value for the regression relationship between total wage and salary employment in Chicago and real GNP is 216.84. Hence the null hypothesis is rejected. Consequently, it is concluded that the regression relationship between NTO1 and RGNP has significant explanatory power.

4.3-5. With one degree of freedom in the numerator and 74 degrees of freedom in the denominator,

$$F_c{}^{.05} = 4.0 \qquad F_c{}^{.01} = 7.08$$

The hypothesis for each equation is

$$H_0: b_1 = 0$$
$$H_1: b_1 \neq 0$$

<u>NMI1, RGNP</u>: Since $F_m = 82.17$ exceeds 7.08, the null hypothesis is rejected and the alternative accepted at the 0.01 level of significance.

<u>NCN1, RGNP</u>: Since $F_m = 2.43$ is less than 4.0, the null hypothesis cannot be rejected at 0.05 level of significance.

<u>NMN1, RGNP</u>: Since $F_m = 167.61$ exceeds 7.08, the null hypothesis is rejected and the alternative accepted at the 0.01 level of significance.

NTR1, RGNP: Since F_m = 40.03 exceeds 7.08, the null hypothesis is rejected and the alternative accepted at the 0.01 level of significance.

NWR1, RGNP: Since F_m = 796.68 exceeds 7.08, the null hypothesis is rejected and the alternative accepted at the 0.01 level of significance.

NFI1, RGNP: Since F_m = 729.85 exceeds 7.08, the null hypothesis is rejected and the alternative accepted at the 0.01 level of significance.

NSR1, RGNP: Since F_m = 903.53 exceeds 7.08, the null hypothesis is rejected and the alternative accepted at the 0.01 level of significance.

NGV1, RGNP: Since F_m = 226.24 exceeds 7.08, the null hypothesis is rejected and the alternative accepted at the 0.01 level of significance.

4.3-6. Given $\widehat{NTO1}_t$ = 126.68 + 2.76 RGNP$_t$

	y_t	$\hat{y}_t$	$(y_t - \hat{y}_t)$	$(y_t - \hat{y}_t)^2$
OBS.	NTO1$_t$	$\widehat{NTO1}_t$	(NTO1$_t$ - $\widehat{NTO1}_t$)	(NTO1$_t$ - $\widehat{NTO1}_t$)^2
1965:1	2,600.3	2,628.90	-28.60	817.96
1965:2	2,681.4	2,664.78	16.62	276.22
1965:3	2,728.1	2,704.52	23.58	556.02
1965:4	2,781.9	2,767.45	14.45	208.80
1966:1	2,738.7	2,818.78	-80.08	6,412.81
1966:2	2,820.3	2,829.82	-9.52	90.63
1966:3	2,870.7	2,853.28	17.42	303.46
1966:4	2,922.7	2,877.57	45.13	2,036.72
Total			-1 *	10,702.62

* Total does not add to zero due to rounding error.

$$s_e = \sqrt{\Sigma(y_t - \hat{y}_t)^2/(n - 2)}$$

$$s_e = \sqrt{10,702.62/6} = 42.23$$

4.3-7. No. The coefficient of variation (cv$_e$) which is a relative measure should be used in comparing the dispersion of residuals between two different regression equations.

4.3-8. >*FETCH NTO1 GNP PDE*
>*GENR RGNP=GNP/PDE*
>*SMPL 65.2 83.4*
>*LS NTO1 C RGNP(-1)*

```
SMPL   1965.2 - 1983.4
75 Observations
LS // Dependent Variable is NTO1
=================================================================
      VARIABLE    COEFFICIENT   STD. ERROR    T-STAT.    2-TAIL SIG.
=================================================================
          C       2305782.7     47662.445    48.377349    0.000
     RGNP(-1)     583.40160     37.754326    15.452576    0.000
=================================================================
R-squared              0.765862   Mean of dependent var    3033848.
Adjusted R-squared     0.762655   S.D. of dependent var    127916.1
S.E. of regression     62318.31   Sum of squared resid     2.84D+11
Durbin-Watson stat     0.563561   F-statistic              238.7821
Log likelihood         -933.4076
=================================================================
                        Covariance Matrix
=================================================================
C,C                    2.27D+09   C,RGNP(-1)               -1778837.
RGNP(-1),RGNP(-1)      1425.389
=================================================================
```

```
=================================================================
          Residual Plot               obs RESIDUAL   ACTUAL    FITTED
=================================================================
|  *       :      |     :    |  65.2 -153296.  2681400  2834696
|    *     :      |     :    |  65.3 -114179.  2728100  2842279
|        *:       |     :    |  65.4  -68787.4 2781900  2850687
|     *    :      |     :    |  66.1 -125268.  2738700  2863968
|         :*      |     :    |  66.2  -54551.7 2820300  2874852
|         :    *| |     :    |  66.3  -6447.60 2870700  2877148
|         :       |  *  :    |  66.4   40562.9 2922700  2882137
|         : *     |     :    |  67.1  -35833.5 2851400  2887233
|         :       |* :  :    |  67.2   11857.6 2899700  2887842
|         :       |   *:     |  67.3   54864.2 2946500  2891636
|         :       |   *       67.4   64023.1 2962700  2898677
|         :    *  |     :    |  68.1    698.386 2905900 2905202
|         :       |   *:     |  68.2   51663.7 2962200  2910536
|         :       |   :*     |  68.3   67885.7 2989600  2921714
|         :       |   :  *   |  68.4   88225.3 3017200  2928975
|         :       |*  :      |  69.1   35461.5 2966600  2931138
|         :       |   : *    |  69.2   86624.2 3024900  2938276
|         :       |   :    * |  69.3  116948.  3057900  2940952
|         :       |   :    * |  69.4  115003.  3057800  2942797
|         :       |* :       |  70.1   42814.9 2981900  2939085
|         :       |* :       |  70.2   39872.3 2976500  2936628
|         :       |   :*     |  70.3   67385.8 3005000  2937614
|         :       |* :       |  70.4   43446.4 2987100  2943654
```

```
|        :  *    |       :      |  71.1  -39537.8   2899000   2938538
|        :     *|       :       |  71.2  -8361.04   2945900   2954261
|        :      |*      :        |  71.3   11599.7   2969000   2957400
|        :      *       :        |  71.4  -62.8384   2962500   2962563
|      *:       |       :        |  72.1  -68497.4   2899700   2968197
|        :   *  |       :        |  72.2  -20502.1   2960400   2980902
|        :      *       :        |  72.3  -2642.54   2990700   2993343
|        :     *|       :        |  72.4  -7949.08   2993900   3001849
|        *      |       :        |  73.1  -60994.3   2953500   3014494
|        :      |*      :        |  73.2   8277.62   3041400   3033122
|        :      |    *:          |  73.3   47054.1   3081100   3034046
|        :      |     :*         |  73.4   70638.1   3109000   3038362
|        :      |*      :        |  74.1   12303.4   3056700   3044397
|        :      |     :*         |  74.2   72515.5   3109500   3036985
|        :      |     :   *      |  74.3   88340.2   3126100   3037760
|        :      |     :  *       |  74.4   84394.2   3117600   3033206
|        :  *   |       :        |  75.1  -42153.4   2981400   3023553
|        :  *   |       :        |  75.2  -37852.3   2970500   3008352
|        :  *   |       :        |  75.3  -43844.3   2973000   3016844
|        :  *   |       :        |  75.4  -45032.1   2987700   3032732
|      *  :      |       :        |  76.1  -107398.   2931900   3039298
|       *:      |       :        |  76.2  -67535.1   2987900   3055435
|        :    *|       :         |  76.3  -11517.1   3049000   3060517
|        :   *  |       :        |  76.4  -19332.6   3045500   3064833
|      *  :      |       :        |  77.1  -111108.   2960500   3071608
|        :   *  |       :        |  77.2  -24657.3   3063600   3088257
|        :   *  |       :        |  77.3  -18724.2   3082400   3101124
|        :      *       :        |  77.4   1237.01   3115500   3114263
|        :*     |       :        |  78.1  -52741.1   3063100   3115841
|        :      |*      :        |  78.2   6946.82   3129500   3122553
|        :      |    *  :        |  78.3   37088.4   3181200   3144112
|        :      |    *  :        |  78.4   32771.6   3183800   3151028
|        :    * |       :        |  79.1  -19149.7   3143300   3162450
|        :      |    *:          |  79.2   47515.8   3212400   3164884
|        :      |     :  *       |  79.3   78983.6   3241900   3162916
|        :      |     :  *       |  79.4   84688.1   3257800   3173112
|        :      |  *   :         |  80.1   20811.7   3195500   3174688
|        :      |    *:          |  80.2   50018.6   3228800   3178781
|        :      |     :*         |  80.3   75429.5   3233800   3158370
|        :      |     *          |  80.4   63592.5   3223600   3160008
|        :      *       :        |  81.1   1919.69   3169900   3167980
|        :      |*      :        |  81.2   5629.49   3192400   3186771
|        :     *|       :        |  81.3  -6087.00   3182100   3188187
|        :   *  |       :        |  81.4  -26234.0   3169700   3195934
|       *  :     |       :        |  82.1  -90415.3   3094500   3184915
|        *:      |       :        |  82.2  -74765.8   3097800   3172566
|       *  :     |       :        |  82.3  -89245.1   3085400   3174645
```

56

```
|    *      :    |        :      | 82.4 -128442.  3044100 3172542
|         *      |        :      | 83.1 -59361.6  3110300 3169662
|         :    * |        :      | 83.2 -19542.1  3155600 3175142
|         :      |  *     :      | 83.3 17499.5   3213000 3195501
|         :      |  *     :      | 83.4 15455.4   3227500 3212045
========================================================================
```

(a) $s_e = 62,318.31$

The following quarters show residuals greater than the estimated standard error: 65:2,   65:3,   65:4,   66:1,   68:3,   68:4,   69:2,   69:3,   69:4, 70:3,   73:4,   74:2,   74:3,   74:4,   76:1,   76:2,   77:1,   79:3,   79:4,   80:3,   82:1, 82:2, 82:3, 82:4.

(b)   To construct the relevant confidence interval, the standard deviation of RGNP is needed.   This can be obtained by running a *COVA* on NTO1 and RGNP(-1).

>*COVA NTO1 RGNP(-1)*

SMPL   1965.2 - 1983.4
75 Observations

Series	Mean	S.D.	Maximum	Minimum
NTO1	3033848.0	127916.15	3257800.0	2681400.0
RGNP(-1)	1247.9658	191.88148	1553.4100	906.60160

	Covariance	Correlation
NTO1,NTO1	1.614D+10	1.0000000
NTO1,RGNP(-1)	21193573.	0.8751355
RGNP(-1),RGNP(-1)	36327.588	1.0000000

From the output:

$$s_e = \sqrt{\frac{\Sigma(x - \bar{x})^2}{n - 2}} = 191.8$$

$$\frac{\Sigma(x - \bar{x})^2}{73} = (119.8)^2 \qquad \Sigma(x - \bar{x})^2 = 2,685,468.52$$

$$s_{ef} = 62,318.31\sqrt{1 + \frac{1}{75} + \frac{(1,571.9 - 1,248.0)^2}{2,685,468.52}} = 63,938.60$$

57

$$\widehat{NTO1} = 2{,}305{,}782.7 + 583.40160(1571.912) = 3{,}222{,}838.7$$

At a 0.05 level of significance, the appropriate confidence interval is

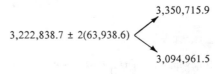

$$3{,}222{,}838.7 \pm 2(63{,}938.6) \quad\begin{array}{l} 3{,}350{,}715.9 \\ \\ 3{,}094{,}961.5 \end{array}$$

(c) At a 0.10 level of significance, the appropriate confidence interval is

$$3{,}222{,}838.7 \pm 1.671(63{,}938.6) \quad\begin{array}{l} 3{,}329{,}680.1 \\ \\ 3{,}115{,}997.3 \end{array}$$

(d) The interval for the 0.05 level of significance is wider than for the 0.10 level of significance since the 0.05 confidence interval represents a higher level of confidence and a correspondingly higher critical t value.

Study Project:

4.3-9. Using equation (3.3-4),

$$r_{y\cdot\hat{y}} = \frac{\Sigma(y_t - \bar{y})\,(\hat{y}_t - \bar{y})/(n-1)}{\sqrt{\Sigma(y_t - \bar{y})^2/(n-1)}\ \ \sqrt{\Sigma\,(\hat{y}_t - \bar{y})^2/(n-1)}}$$

Multiplying the numerator and denominator by $n-1$ and using the summation that $\Sigma(y_t - \bar{y})\,(\hat{y}_t - \bar{y}) = \Sigma(\hat{y}_t - \bar{y})y_t$, the above expression is equal to

$$r_{y\cdot\hat{y}} = \frac{\Sigma(\hat{y}_t - \bar{y})y_t}{\sqrt{\Sigma(y_t - \bar{y})^2}\ \ \sqrt{\Sigma\,(\hat{y}_t - \bar{y})^2}}$$

Since $y_t = \hat{y}_t + \hat{e}_t$, the numerator in the above expression is equivalent to

$$\Sigma(\hat{y}_t - \bar{y})\,(\hat{y}_t + \hat{e})$$

But using the error term assumptions $\Sigma\hat{y}_t\hat{e}_t = 0$ and $\Sigma\hat{e} = 0$, the above expression is equal to

$$\Sigma(\hat{y}_t - \bar{y})\,\hat{y}_t$$

58

and using the reverse of the above summation operation,

$$\Sigma(\hat{y}_t - \bar{y})\,\hat{y}_t = \Sigma(\hat{y}_t - \bar{y})\,(\hat{y}_t - \bar{y}) = \Sigma(\hat{y}_t - \bar{y})^2$$

Therefore,

$$r_{y \cdot \hat{y}} = \frac{\Sigma(\hat{y}_t - \bar{y})^2}{\sqrt{\Sigma(y_t - \bar{y})^2}\ \sqrt{\Sigma\,(\hat{y}_t - \bar{y})^2}}$$

Squaring $r_{y \cdot \hat{y}}$ results in

$$[r_{y \cdot \hat{y}}]^2 = R^2 = \frac{\Sigma(\hat{y}_t - \bar{y})^4}{\sqrt{\Sigma(y_t - \bar{y})^2}\ \sqrt{\Sigma\,(\hat{y}_t - \bar{y})^2}} = \frac{\Sigma(\hat{y}_t - \bar{y})^2}{\Sigma(y_t - \bar{y})^2}$$

The above expression is the same as that given in (4.3-3) in the text as the formula for R^2.

4.4 Exercises

Questions for Review:

4.4-1. The t statistic is used to standardize for different measures of $\hat{b}_1$. If such a standardization is not used, there will be a different probability distribution of $\hat{b}_1$ for different tests depending on the units of measure for x and y.

4.4-2. Since the measured t statistic, $t_m = (\hat{b}_1 - b_1)/s\hat{b}_1$, is based on both $\hat{b}_1$ and its standard error, and since the normality assumption, $e_t(N(O,\sigma_e^2))$, made it possible to infer that the sampling distributions of $\hat{b}_0$ and $\hat{b}_1$ were normal, it follows that the t distribution is also normal.

4.4-3.

	y_t	x_t	$x_t - \bar{x}$	$(x_t - \bar{x})^2$
OBS.	NTO1	RGNP	RGNP - $\overline{\text{RGNP}}$	(RGNP - $\overline{\text{RGNP}}$)^2
1965:1	2,600.3	906.6	-50.4	2,540.16
1965:2	2,681.4	911.6	-45.4	2,061.16
1965:3	2,728.1	934.0	-23.0	529.00
1965:4	2,781.9	956.8	-0.2	0.04
1966:1	2,738.7	975.4	18.4	338.56
1966:2	2,820.3	979.4	22.4	501.76
1966:3	2,870.7	987.9	30.9	954.81
1966:4	2,922.7	996.7	39.7	1,576.09
Total				8,501.58

$\bar{x} = \overline{\text{RGNP}} = 957$

$s_e = 42.23$

$s_{\hat{b}_1} = s_e / \sqrt{(x_t - \bar{x})^2}$

$s_{\hat{b}_1} = 42.23 / \sqrt{8,501.58} = 42.23 / 92.20 = .46$

As a result of rounding error, there is a slight difference between the manual computation and the computer result.

4.4-4.

$$H_0: b_1 \leq 0$$
$$H_1: b_1 > 0$$

$$t_m = \hat{b}_1 / s_{\hat{b}_1} = 606.72 / 41.20 = 14.73$$

At a 0.01 level of significance and 74 degrees of freedom (76-2), the critical t value for a one-tailed test is 2.326. Since 14.73 > 2.326, the null hypothesis is rejected, and it is concluded that b_1 is significantly greater than zero.   The probability of making a Type I error is 0.01. That is, there is a one percent chance that the null hypothesis is incorrectly being rejected.

4.4-5.   (a) $H_0: b_1 \leq 0$ (c) $H_0: b_1 \geq 0$
                  $H_1: b_1 > 0$ $H_1: b_1 < 0$

         (b) $H_0: b_1 \leq 0$ (d) $H_0: b_1 = 0$
                  $H_1: b_1 > 0$ $H_1: b_1 \neq 0$

Computer Exercises:

4.4-6.   >*FETCH BTO GEX TFG AAA PDE*
              >*SMPL 65.1 83.4*
              >*GENR DEF=GEX-TFG*
              >*GENR RDEF=DEF/PDE*

              [Generate RAAAR as described in Computer Session 3.1-4.]

              >*LS RAAAR C RDEF*

```
SMPL  1965.1 - 1983.4
76 Observations
LS // Dependent Variable is RAAAR
=====================================================================
     VARIABLE   COEFFICIENT   STD. ERROR    T-STAT.   2-TAIL SIG.
=====================================================================
        C        2.5705560    0.2023431    12.703944    0.000
      RDEF       0.0162819    0.0057986     2.8079091   0.007
---------------------------------------------------------------------
R-squared              0.096286    Mean of dependent var   2.967327
Adjusted R-squared     0.084074    S.D. of dependent var   1.319274
S.E. of regression     1.262598    Sum of squared resid    117.9673
Durbin-Watson stat     0.160295    F-statistic             7.884354
Log likelihood       -124.5470
=====================================================================
```

>*LS BTO C RAAAR*

```
SMPL  1965.1 - 1983.4
76 Observations
LS // Dependent Variable is BTO
=====================================================================
     VARIABLE   COEFFICIENT   STD. ERROR    T-STAT.   2-TAIL SIG.
=====================================================================
        C        279671.84    37073.958     7.5436197   0.000
      RAAAR     -4228.6408    11428.973    -0.3699931   0.713
---------------------------------------------------------------------
R-squared              0.001847    Mean of dependent var   267124.1
Adjusted R-squared    -0.011642    S.D. of dependent var   129825.3
S.E. of regression     130578.8    Sum of squared resid    1.26D+12
Durbin-Watson stat     0.487252    F-statistic             0.136895
Log likelihood       -1002.086
=====================================================================
```

(a)

$$H_0: b_1 = 0$$
$$H_1: b_1 \neq 0$$

At a 0.05 level of significance and 74 degrees of freedom (76-2), the critical t value for a two-tailed test is 2.0. Since $t_m = 2.8079$ is greater than 2.0, the null hypothesis is rejected. This implies that the real federal government spending deficit has a significant impact on the real AAA rate.

(b)

$$H_0: b_1 \geq 0$$
$$H_0: b_1 < 0$$

At a 0.10 level of significance and 74 degrees of freedom (76-2), the critical t value for a one-tailed test is -1.296. t_m = -0.369 is greater than -1.296.   Hence, the null hypothesis cannot be rejected. This suggests there is not significant evidence at the 0.10 level of significance that the movement in the real AAA rate during a given quarter affects building valuation.

4.4-7.   >*FETCH BTO NCN BTO1 NCN1 PRR MNS PDE*
>*GENR RMNS=MNS/PDE*
>*SMPL 66.1 83.4*
>*GENR PRMNS=((RMNS-RMNS(-4))/RMNS(-4))*100*
>*SMPL 65.2 83.4*
>*LS NCN C BTO(-1)*

```
SMPL  1965.2 - 1983.4
75 Observations
LS // Dependent Variable is NCN
===================================================================
      VARIABLE   COEFFICIENT   STD. ERROR    T-STAT.   2-TAIL SIG.
===================================================================
         C        15002.036    1464.1964    10.245918    0.000
      BTO(-1)      0.0567081    0.0049704    11.409144    0.000
===================================================================
R-squared            0.640692   Mean of dependent var   30032.51
Adjusted R-squared   0.635770   S.D. of dependent var   9169.378
S.E. of regression   5533.851   Sum of squared resid    2.24D+09
Durbin-Watson stat   0.790726   F-statistic             130.1686
Log likelihood       -751.8048
===================================================================
```

>*LS NCN1 C BTO1(-1)*

```
SMPL  1965.2 - 1983.4
75 Observations
LS // Dependent Variable is NCN1
===================================================================
      VARIABLE   COEFFICIENT   STD. ERROR    T-STAT.   2-TAIL SIG.
===================================================================
         C        112895.22    3991.2514    28.285669    0.000
      BTO1(-1)     0.0097256    0.0208955    0.4654380    0.643
===================================================================
R-squared            0.002959   Mean of dependent var   114622.4
Adjusted R-squared  -0.010699   S.D. of dependent var   12658.17
S.E. of regression   12725.71   Sum of squared resid    1.18D+10
Durbin-Watson stat   1.030332   F-statistic             0.216633
Log likelihood       -814.2603
===================================================================
```

>*SMPL 66.2 83.4*
>*LS PRR C PRMNS(-1)*

```
SMPL  1966.2 - 1983.4
71 Observations
LS // Dependent Variable is PRR
=====================================================================
      VARIABLE   COEFFICIENT   STD. ERROR    T-STAT.   2-TAIL SIG.
=====================================================================
         C        9.4336488    0.4480904    21.053006    0.000
     PRMNS(-1)   -0.4625166    0.1611000    -2.8709903   0.006
=====================================================================
R-squared              0.106710   Mean of dependent var   9.291718
Adjusted R-squared     0.093764   S.D. of dependent var   3.941984
S.E. of regression     3.752628   Sum of squared resid    971.6728
Durbin-Watson stat     0.192943   F-statistic             8.242585
Log likelihood      -193.6247
=====================================================================
```

>*SMPL 67.1 83.4*
>*LS PRR C PRMNS(-4)*

```
SMPL  1967.1 - 1983.4
68 Observations
LS // Dependent Variable is PRR
=====================================================================
      VARIABLE   COEFFICIENT   STD. ERROR    T-STAT.   2-TAIL SIG.
=====================================================================
         C        9.4533622    0.4699066    20.117536    0.000
     PRMNS(-4)   -0.3809821    0.1932315    -1.9716352   0.053
=====================================================================
R-squared              0.055623   Mean of dependent var   9.446000
Adjusted R-squared     0.041314   S.D. of dependent var   3.957438
S.E. of regression     3.874827   Sum of squared resid    990.9425
Durbin-Watson stat     0.148624   F-statistic             3.887345
Log likelihood      -187.5789
=====================================================================
```

>*SAVE WF4-4-7*

Critical t Values

Level of Significance	t_c
0.01	2.390
0.05	1.671
0.10	1.296

63

(a)

$$H_0: b_1 \leq 0$$
$$H_1: b_1 > 0$$

$t_m = 11.41$ $n = 75$ $df = 73$

Since t_m is greater than the critical t values at all three levels of significance, the null hypothesis is rejected. Therefore, it is concluded that lagged building valuation positively influences construction employment in Orange County.

(b)

$$H_0: b_1 \leq 0$$
$$H1: b_1 > 0$$

$t_m = 0.465$ $n = 75$ $df = 73$

Since t_m is less than the critical t values at all three levels of significance, the null hypothesis cannot be rejected. Therefore, it is concluded that lagged building valuation in Chicago does not have a significant positive impact on Chicago's construction employment.

(c)

$$H_0: b_1 \geq 0$$
$$H1: b_1 < 0$$

$t_m = -2.87$ $n = 75$ $df = 73$

Since $|t_m|$ is greater than the critical t values at all three levels of significance, the null hypothesis is rejected. Therefore, it is concluded that the annual percentage changes in the real money supply in the prior quarter does influence the nominal prime interest rate.

(d)

$$H_0: b_1 = 0$$
$$H1: b_1 \neq 0$$

$t_m = -1.97$ $n = 75$ $df = 73$

At the 0.01 ~~and 0.05~~ levels of significance the null hypothesis cannot be rejected, but it is rejected at the 0.10 level. The annual percentage changes in the real money supply lagged four quarters influence the current nominal prime interest rate at the 10 percent significance level. There is not, however, enough statistical evidence to support this hypothesis at a higher level of confidence

64

(0.95 or 0.99).

4.5 Exercises

Questions for Review:

4.5-1. H_0: $b_1 = b_2 = ... = b_k = 0$ for a multiple linear regression equation with k independent variables.

H_0: $b_1 = 0$ when testing the significance of a specific regression coefficient.

4.5-2. $\overline{R}^2$ adjusts for the loss in degrees of freedom caused by adding more independent variables in an equation.   As a result, $\overline{R}^2$ is often used as an alternative to the R^2 value that includes no such adjustment.

4.5-3. $\widehat{NTO}_t = -562,090.5 + 1,569.0\ RCUN_{t-1} + 349.2\ RGTO_{t-1} - 572.9\ RGTO_{t-1}$

$+ 1135.4\ RBAL_{t-1}$

$= -562,090.5 + 1,569.0(1,018.4) + 349.2(237.7) - 572.9(319.5)$

$+ 1,135.4(-8.6)$

$= -562,090.5 + 1,597,869.6 + 83,004.8 - 183,041.6 - 9,764.4$

$= 925,977.9$

Using equation (4.5-16) to forecast $NTO_{84:1}$ results in 925,977.9 instead of the 950,000 estimate when equation (4.5-14) is used.

Computer Exercises:

4.5-4.   >*FETCH NTO1 GNP PDE TFG TSL*
>*SMPL 65.1 83.4*
>*GENR TTO=TFG+TSL*
>*GENR RTTO=TTO/PDE*
>*GENR RGNP=GNP/PDE*
>*LS NTO1 C RGNP RTTO*

65

```
SMPL  1965.1 - 1983.4
76 Observations
LS // Dependent Variable is NTO1
```

VARIABLE	COEFFICIENT	STD. ERROR	T-STAT.	2-TAIL SIG.
C	2507535.2	91938.972	27.273909	0.000
RGNP	-299.46437	296.31981	-1.0106121	0.316
RTTO	2118.2522	686.63397	3.0849802	0.003

R-squared	0.774913	Mean of dependent var	3028143.
Adjusted R-squared	0.768746	S.D. of dependent var	136446.3
S.E. of regression	65615.45	Sum of squared resid	3.14D+11
Durbin-Watson stat	0.642257	F-statistic	125.6595
Log likelihood	-949.2680		

Level of significance = 0.01　　$t_c = 2.326$　　df = 74

H_0: $b_1 \leq 0$　　　　　　　　　　H_0: $b_2 \geq 0$
H_1: $b_1 > 0$　　　　　　　　　　H1: $b_2 < 0$

Since $|t_m| = -1.01 < 2.326$, 　　Since $|t_m| = 3.08 > 2.326$,
do not reject H_0.　　　　　　　reject H_0 and accept H_1.

4.5-5.　　　　>*FETCH CUN DSY AAA*
　　　　　　　　>*SMPL 65.1 83.4*
　　　　　　　　>*LS CUN C DSY AAA*

```
SMPL  1965.1 - 1983.4
76 Observations
LS // Dependent Variable is CUN
```

VARIABLE	COEFFICIENT	STD. ERROR	T-STAT.	2-TAIL SIG.
C	5.8458090	5.1910985	1.1261218	0.264
DSY	0.9490068	0.0056353	168.40298	0.000
AAA	-6.2460129	1.2238211	-5.1036976	0.000

R-squared	0.999617	Mean of dependent var	1054.113
Adjusted R-squared	0.999607	S.D. of dependent var	542.6438
S.E. of regression	10.76018	Sum of squared resid	8452.050
Durbin-Watson stat	0.923459	F-statistic	95335.70
Log likelihood	-286.8737		

4.5-6.   >*FETCH NTO GNP PDE TFG TSL*
           >*SMPL 65.1 83.4*
           >*GENR TTO=TFG + TSL*
           >*GENR RTTO=TT0/PDE*
           >*GENR RGNP=GNP/PDE*
           >*SMPL 65.2 83.4*
           >*LS NTO C RGNP(-1) RTTO(-1)*

```
SMPL  1965.2 - 1983.4
75 Observations
LS // Dependent Variable is NTO
===================================================================
        VARIABLE   COEFFICIENT   STD. ERROR    T-STAT.   2-TAIL SIG.
===================================================================
           C      -802027.94     32051.917    -25.022776   0.000
        RGNP(-1)   1493.3190     102.56355     14.559939   0.000
        RTTO(-1)  -1124.0264     235.87392     -4.7653697  0.000
===================================================================
R-squared             0.988340   Mean of dependent var    587941.4
Adjusted R-squared    0.988016   S.D. of dependent var    195007.4
S.E. of regression    21347.40   Sum of squared resid     3.28D+10
Durbin-Watson stat    0.637432   F-statistic              3051.471
Log likelihood        -852.5419
===================================================================
                        Covariance Matrix
===================================================================
C,C                   1.03D+09   C,RGNP(-1)               -3015033.
C,RTTO(-1)            6505797.   RGNP(-1),RGNP(-1)         10519.28
RGNP(-1),RTTO(-1)    -23998.96   RTTO(-1),RTTO(-1)         55636.50
===================================================================


===================================================================
        Residual Plot              obs RESIDUAL ACTUAL   FITTED
===================================================================
|        :    |    :    *  | 65.2  44509.3  298750.  254241.
|        :    |    :  *    | 65.3  32686.2  302780.  270094.
|        :    |  *:        | 65.4  15900.4  308650.  292750.
|        :  * |    :       | 66.1  -6917.35 312730.  319647.
|        :    *    :       | 66.2  -243.372 331450.  331693.
|        :    |*   :       | 66.3  7556.58  337640.  330083.
|        :    |*   :       | 66.4  2889.30  340350.  337461.
|        :  * |    :       | 67.1  -9100.60 338760.  347861.
|        :    |  * :       | 67.2  9857.61  357130.  347272.
|        :    |  * :       | 67.3  8250.16  364300.  356050.
|        :    |* :         | 67.4  5101.81  371630.  366528.
|        :   *|    :       | 68.1  -3859.29 371430.  375289.
|        :    |  * :       | 68.2  7188.84  384830.  377641.
```

67

```
|              :   *  |      :       |  68.3  -8453.14   390060.   398513.
|              :   *|        :       |  68.4  -4916.22   396227.   401143.
|              :   *|        :       |  69.1  -4447.64   396360.   400808.
|              :      | *    :       |  69.2   8042.22   415040.   406998.
|              :      | *    :       |  69.3   7588.14   418200.   410612.
|              :      |*     :       |  69.4   3361.27   422690.   419329.
|              :      |   *: |       |  70.1   14412.1   423370.   408958.
|              :      |    :*         |  70.2   22783.4   431870.   409087.
|              :      |   *: |       |  70.3   15086.3   425510.   410424.
|              :   *  |      :       |  70.4  -8513.18   420300.   428813.
|              :    * |      :       |  71.1  -1558.65   417100.   418659.
|            *        |      :       |  71.2  -18839.1   433830.   452669.
|             :*      |      :       |  71.3  -17052.8   439290.   456343.
|          *:         |      :       |  71.4  -24627.3   442470.   467097.
|             :*      |      :       |  72.1  -15180.0   458710.   473890.
|              :    * |      :       |  72.2  -1901.67   480900.   482802.
|             :*      |      :       |  72.3  -17293.1   485210.   502503.
|        *     :      |      :       |  72.4  -31544.8   495830.   527375.
|         *    :      |      :       |  73.1  -28651.7   509716.   538368.
|       *      :      |      :       |  73.2  -36788.7   538170.   574959.
|       *      :      |      :       |  73.3  -37702.8   542370.   580073.
|      *       :      |      :       |  73.4  -45462.1   548120.   593582.
|   *          :      |      :       |  74.1  -58794.3   547060.   605854.
|              :  *   |      :       |  74.2  -12458.8   571990.   584449.
|              :  *   |      :       |  74.3  -10407.9   571680.   582088.
|              :      | *    :       |  74.4   6864.31   573630.   566766.
|              :   *| :       |  75.1  -2697.95   550420.   553118.
|              :      |      :   *   |  75.2   38864.8   566660.   527795.
|              :   *| :       |  75.3  -5563.71   571520.   577084.
|              :      | *    :       |  75.4   9212.68   586670.   577457.
|              :      *      :       |  76.1   301.995   590200.   589898.
|              :      *      :       |  76.2  -1750.60   615790.   617541.
|              :   *  |      :       |  76.3  -9605.10   614730.   624335.
|              :      |   *  :       |  76.4   10943.2   639770.   628827.
|              :      | *    :       |  77.1   8148.48   647130.   638982.
|              :      | *    :       |  77.2   12807.6   680570.   667762.
|              : *    |      :       |  77.3  -10178.6   686380.   696559.
|              : *    |      :       |  77.4  -13595.6   710660.   724256.
|              :   *| :       |  78.1  -2303.87   722130.   724434.
|              :      |      *       |  78.2   20817.1   756893.   736076.
|             :*      |      :       |  78.3  -14769.9   760207.   774977.
|              :   *  |      :       |  78.4  -8393.81   783726.   792120.
|          *   :      |      :       |  79.1  -27954.9   784300.   812255.
|             :*      |      :       |  79.2  -17365.2   799330.   816695.
|              :   *| :       |  79.3  -3101.92   811736.   814838.
|              :      |*     :       |  79.4   3755.08   838897.   835142.
|              :   *| :       |  80.1  -4428.93   831467.   835896.
```

68

```
|           :    *    :          |  80.2  1078.08  844370.  843292.
|           :    |    :   *      |  80.3  31282.7  837933.  806650.
|           :    |    :       *  |  80.4  54221.5  857137.  802916.
|           :    |    :      *   |  81.1  46158.8  860133.  813974.
|           :    |    :  *       |  81.2  33028.3  876927.  843899.
|           :    |    :*         |  81.3  22291.4  872731.  850440.
|           :    |  * :          |  81.4  6043.87  877296.  871252.
|           :    *    :          |  82.1  1123.99  861402.  860278.
|           :    |    :  *       |  82.2  27225.4  866060.  838835.
|           :    |*   :          |  82.3  2164.47  846726.  844562.
|           :    |  * :          |  82.4  6690.35  851627.  844937.
|           :    |  *  :         |  83.1  11240.1  851330.  840090.
|           :    |    :*         |  83.2  25199.5  875425.  850225.
|           :*   |    :          |  83.3 -14615.7  868058.  882674.
|      *    :    |    :          |  83.4 -43637.2  883132.  926769.
===================================================================
```

OLNTO and differences between NTO and OLNTO between 83.1 to 83.4 can now be generated. A comparison of the above residuals to the generated differences for the same periods shows they are equal.

>*SMPL 83.1 83.4*
>*FORCST OLNTO*
>*GENR DIFF=NTO-OLNTO*
>*PRINT RESID DIFF*

```
================================
  obs     RESID       DIFF
================================
1983.1   11240.13    11240.13
1983.2   25199.50    25199.50
1983.3  -14615.69   -14615.69
1983.4  -43637.19   -43637.19
================================
```

4.5-7.   >*FETCH NTO PDE GNP*
          >*GENR RGNP=GNP/PDE*
          >*LS NTO C RGNP(-1)*

69

```
SMPL  1965.2 - 1983.4
75 Observations
LS // Dependent Variable is NTO
====================================================================
      VARIABLE    COEFFICIENT   STD. ERROR    T-STAT.   2-TAIL SIG.
====================================================================
         C        -670591.08    18597.082    -36.058941   0.000
      RGNP(-1)     1008.4671    14.731101     68.458366    0.000
====================================================================
R-squared              0.984662   Mean of dependent var   587941.4
Adjusted R-squared     0.984452   S.D. of dependent var   195007.4
S.E. of regression     24315.55   Sum of squared resid    4.32D+10
Durbin-Watson stat     0.349172   F-statistic             4686.548
Log likelihood        -862.8222
====================================================================
```

>*EXPAND 65.1 84.1*
>*SMPL 84.1 84.1*
>*FORCST OLNTO*
>*PRINT OLNTO*

```
===================
  obs      OLNTO
===================
1984.1   914630.5
===================
```

Except for rounding error, the computer generated forecast is equal to the manually calculated value.

4.5-8.   >*FETCH NTO1 GNP PDE TFG TSL*
>*SMPL 65.1 83.4*
>*GENR TTO=TFG+TSL*
>*GENR RTTO=TTO/PDE*
>*GENR RGNP=GNP/PDE*
>*SMPL 65.2 83.4*
>*LS NTO1 C RGNP(-1) RTTO(-1)*

```
SMPL   1965.2 - 1983.4
75 Observations
LS // Dependent Variable is NTO1
=====================================================================
      VARIABLE    COEFFICIENT   STD. ERROR    T-STAT.   2-TAIL SIG.
=====================================================================
         C         2516247.7    89696.358    28.052953    0.000
      RGNP(-1)    -192.97376    287.02110    -0.6723330   0.504
      RTTO(-1)     1799.8619    660.08630     2.7267069   0.008
=====================================================================
R-squared              0.787777   Mean of dependent var    3033848.
Adjusted R-squared     0.781882   S.D. of dependent var    127916.1
S.E. of regression     59740.84   Sum of squared resid     2.57D+11
Durbin-Watson stat     0.637461   F-statistic              133.6328
Log likelihood        -929.7224
=====================================================================
```

>*EXPAND 65.1 84.4*
>*DATA RGNP RTTO*

OBS.	RGNP	RTTO
1965.2	*N84.1*	
1984.1	*1595*	*533*
1984.2	*1601*	*550*
1984.3	*1616*	*579*
1984.4	*END*	

>*SMPL 84.2 84.4*
>*FORCST OLNTO1*
>*PRINT OLNTO1*

```
====================
  obs      OLNTO1
====================
 1984.2   3167781.
 1984.3   3197221.
 1984.4   3246522.
====================
```

>*PLOT(A) OLNTO1*

71

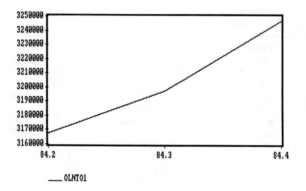

_____ OLNT01

4.5-9.   Fetch and generate all the necessary data.

>_SMPL 65.2 83.4_
>_LS NTO1 C RCUN(-1) RITO(-1) RGTO(-1) RBAL(-1)_

```
SMPL  1965.2 - 1983.4
75 Observations
LS // Dependent Variable is NTO1
=====================================================================
        VARIABLE    COEFFICIENT   STD. ERROR     T-STAT.   2-TAIL SIG.
=====================================================================
           C         2126320.5    56827.094    37.417371     0.000
        RCUN(-1)    -1404.6825    294.39804    -4.7713720    0.000
        RITO(-1)     3797.4245    507.68250     7.4799199    0.000
        RGTO(-1)     4887.0248    771.82321     6.3317930    0.000
        RBAL(-1)     901.22998    874.86069     1.0301411    0.307

---------------------------------------------------------------------
R-squared              0.857630   Mean of dependent var    3033848.
Adjusted R-squared     0.849494   S.D. of dependent var    127916.1
S.E. of regression     49625.14   Sum of squared resid     1.72D+11
Durbin-Watson stat     1.167887   F-statistic              105.4190
Log likelihood         -914.7521
=====================================================================
```

Since the absolute values of t_m for the coefficients of RCUN(-1), RITO(-1) and RGTO(-1) are greater than 2, it is concluded that they are significant at the 0.05 level of significance.   RBAL(-1), however, is not significant since $t_m = 1.03 < 2$.

Given:

$$RCUN_{83:4} = 1,018.43 \qquad RTTO_{83:4} = 236.7494$$

$$RGTO_{83:4} = 319.4768 \qquad RBAL_{83:4} = -8.551704$$

Then:

$$NTO1_{84:1} = 2,126,320.5 - 1,404.6825(1,018.43) + 3,797.4245(236.7494)$$

$$+ 4,887.0248(319.4768) + 901.22998(-8.851704)$$

$$NTO1_{84:1} = 2,126,320.5 - 1,430,570.8 + 899,037.97 + 1,561,291$$

$$- 7,977.421$$

$$= 3,148,101.2$$

Study Projects:

4.5-10.   Goal: MIN $\Sigma(y_t - \hat{y}_t)^2$ or

L.S. $= \Sigma(y_t - \hat{b}_0 - \hat{b}_1(x_{1t}) - \hat{b}_2(x_{2t}))^2$

$$\frac{\partial LS}{\partial \hat{b}_0} = \Sigma - 2(y_t - \hat{b}_0 - \hat{b}_1(x_{1t}) - \hat{b}_2(x_{2t})) = 0$$

$$= \Sigma y_t - n\hat{b}_0 - \hat{b}_1 \Sigma x_{1t} - \hat{b}_2 x_{2t} = 0$$

E1 $\therefore \Sigma y_t = n\hat{b}_0 + \hat{b}_1 \Sigma x_{1t} + \hat{b}_2 \Sigma x_{2t}$

$$\frac{\partial LS}{\partial \hat{b}_1} = \Sigma - 2x_{1t}(y_t - \hat{b}_0 - \hat{b}_1(x_{1t}) - \hat{b}_2(x_{2t})) = 0$$

$$= \Sigma x_{1t} y_t - \hat{b}_0 \Sigma x_{1t} - \hat{b}_1 \Sigma x_{1t}^2 - \hat{b}_2 \Sigma(x_{1t} x_{2t}) = 0$$

E2 $\therefore \Sigma x_{1t} y_t = \hat{b}_0 \Sigma x_{1t} + \hat{b}_1 \Sigma x_{1t}^2 + \hat{b}_2 \Sigma(x_{1t} x_{2t})$

$$\frac{\partial LS}{\partial \hat{b}_2} = \Sigma - 2x_{2t}(y_t - \hat{b}_0 - \hat{b}_1(x_{1t}) - \hat{b}_2(x_{2t})) = 0$$

$$= \Sigma x_{2t} y_t - \hat{b}_0 \Sigma x_{2t} - \hat{b}_1(\Sigma x_{2t} x_{1t}) - \hat{b}_2(\Sigma x_{2t}^2) = 0$$

E3 $\therefore \Sigma x_{2t} y_t = \hat{b}_0 \Sigma x_{2t} + \hat{b}_1(\Sigma x_{2t} x_{1t}) + \hat{b}_2 \Sigma x_{2t}^2$

Note that E1, E2 and E3 equal equation (4.5-4) and the first two equations in (4.5-5) as derived using the instrumental variables technique.

4.5-11. Start a new session over the 1965:1 to 1984:4 sample period. Add the actual values for GNP, TTO and PDE as listed below. Generate the necessary variables, run the regression and forecast NTO1 (OLNTO1).

	GNP	PDE	TTO
84:1	3,560.3	2.21	1,237.7
84:2	3,638.6	2.22	1,260.5
84:3	3,684.8	2.24	1,272.1

>*FETCH NTO1 GNP TFG TSL PDE*
>*GENR TTO=TFG+TSL*
>*DATA GNP PDE TTO*

[Update data to 84:3]

>*GENR RGNP=GNP/PDE*
>*GENR RTTO=TTO/PDE*
>*SMPL 65.2 83.4*
>*LS NTO1 C RGNP(-1) RTTO(-1)*

```
SMPL  1965.2 - 1983.4
75 Observations
LS // Dependent Variable is NTO1
=====================================================================
     VARIABLE    COEFFICIENT    STD. ERROR    T-STAT.    2-TAIL SIG.
=====================================================================
          C      2516247.7      89696.358     28.052953    0.000
    RGNP(-1)     -192.97376     287.02110     -0.6723330   0.504
    RTTO(-1)     1799.8619      660.08630     2.7267069    0.008
=====================================================================
R-squared            0.787777    Mean of dependent var    3033848.
Adjusted R-squared   0.781882    S.D. of dependent var    127916.1
S.E. of regression   59740.84    Sum of squared resid     2.57D+11
Durbin-Watson stat   0.637461    F-statistic              133.6328
Log likelihood       -929.7224
=====================================================================
```

>*SMPL 84.2 84.4*
>*FORCST OLNTO1*
>*PRINT OLNTO1*

```
====================
  obs      OLNTO1
====================
 1984.2    3213372.
 1984.3    3221911.
 1984.4    3221020.
====================
```

4.5-12. Matrix algebra is useful in solving the system of equations following Table 4.5-1.

Note, if

$$A = \begin{vmatrix} a_{11} & a_{12} & a_{13} & a_{11} & a_{12} \\ a_{21} & a_{22} & a_{23} & a_{21} & a_{22} \\ a_{31} & a_{32} & a_{33} & a_{31} & a_{31} \end{vmatrix}$$

$|A| = a_{11}a_{22}a_{33} + a_{12}a_{23}a_{31} + a_{13}a_{21}a_{31} - a_{31}a_{22}a_{13} - a_{31}a_{23}a_{11}$

$- a_{33}a_{21}a_{12}$

$$\hat{b}_0 = \frac{\begin{vmatrix} 2,520.2 & 7,656.4 & 2,253.7 \\ 2,416,242.0 & 7,335,396.9 & 2,160,290.4 \\ 711,954.6 & 2,160,290.4 & 636,511.7 \end{vmatrix}}{|D|} = \frac{-913,489,920}{9,596,992} = -95.185$$

$$|D| = \begin{vmatrix} 8.0 & 7,656.4 & ,253.7 \\ 7,656.4 & 7,335,396.9 & 2,160,290.4 \\ 2,253.7 & 2,160,290.4 & 636,511.7 \end{vmatrix} = 9,596,992$$

$$\hat{b}_1 = \frac{\begin{vmatrix} 8.0 & 2,520.2 & 2,253.7 \\ 7,565.4 & 2,416,242.0 & 2,160,290.4 \\ 2,253.7 & 711,954.6 & 636,511.7 \end{vmatrix}}{|D|} = \frac{1,678,400}{9,596,992} = 0.174888$$

$$\hat{b}_2 = \frac{\begin{vmatrix} 8.0 & 7,656.4 & 2,520.2 \\ 7,656.4 & 7,335,396.9 & 2,416,242.0 \\ 2,253.7 & 2,160,290.4 & 711,954.6 \end{vmatrix}}{|D|} = \frac{8,242,880}{9,596,992} = 0.858902$$

75

5.1 Exercises

Questions for Review:

5.1-1. If x_{1t} and x_{2t} are two independent variables being used to explain y_t, then u_{jt} or u_{1t} is the error term that results in an equation where x_{2t} (regressor) is used to explain x_{1t} (regressand).

5.1-2. x_{1t} is a perfect linear combination of x_{2t} (i.e., $x_{1t} = 2x_{2t}$). As a result, $\hat{u}_{1t}$ will equal zero and it would, therefore, not be possible to solve for $\hat{b}_1$ or $s_{\hat{b}_1}$.

5.1-3. As presented in equation (5.1-6), the standard error of the $\hat{b}_j$ coefficient is

$$s_{\hat{b}_j} = \frac{s_e}{\sqrt{\Sigma \hat{u}_{jt}^2}}$$

When multicollinearity is present in an equation, the Σu_{jt}^2 term in the above equation will be reduced. This occurs because there is a lower level of unexplained variation in x_{jt} when x_{jt} is regressed against a highly collinear variable. As a result, a low $\Sigma \hat{u}_{jt}^2$ leads to a higher standard error of $\hat{b}$ and a corresponding low measured t value, $t_{m,j}$. Thus, even if x_j is a significant variable, multicollinearity will lead to low measured t's and increase the probability of incorrectly accepting the null hypothesis (H_0: $b_j = 0$).

5.1-4. Symptoms of multicollinearity:

    a. When an equation has a high R^2 and low measured t's for its parameter estimates.

    b. A sharp increase in the t statistics for some explanatory variables when one or more of the other variables are deleted from the equation.

    c. When the correlation between two explanatory variables ($r_{x_1 \cdot x_2}$) is greater than the correlation of either of two variables with the dependent variable ($r_{y \cdot x_1}$ or $r_{y \cdot x_2}$).

5.1-5. The higher standard errors and lower t_m statistics associated with multicollinearity result in greater variation of the $\hat{b}$ estimate around the true b values. The resulting lack of precision invalidates the significance tests of the $\hat{b}$ estimates affected by multicollinearity.

5.1-6. If regression equations affected by multicollinearity are used in forecasting, it is important to assume that the collinear relationships that existed among the variables during the estimation period remain during the forecast period.

5.1-7.   Four techniques to reduce multicollinearity:

    a.   Dropping collinear variables.
    b.   Increasing the sample size.
    c.   Respecifying the equation.
    d.   Transforming the variables from levels to first differences or percentage changes. (This is an extension of respecifying the equation.)

Computer Exercises:

5.1-8.   Start up the system using the *CREATE* command and choose the undated data mode.

    >*DATA Y X1 X2*

    [Enter the data for Y, X1 and X2]

    >*LS Y C X1 X2*

    Near singular matrix

5.1-9.   >*FETCH NTO1 GNP PDE TFG TSL*
    >*GENR TTO=TFG+TSL*
    >*GENR RTTO=TTO/PDE*
    >*GENR RGNP=GNP/PDE*
    >*SMPL 65.2 83.4*
    >*LS NTO1 C RGNP(-1) RTTO(-1)*

```
SMPL  1965.2 - 1983.4
75 Observations
LS // Dependent Variable is NTO1
=====================================================================
      VARIABLE   COEFFICIENT   STD. ERROR    T-STAT.    2-TAIL SIG.
=====================================================================
         C        2516247.7    89696.358    28.052953     0.000
     RGNP(-1)    -192.97376    287.02110    -0.6723330     0.504
     RTTO(-1)     1799.8619    660.08630     2.7267069     0.008
=====================================================================
R-squared             0.787777   Mean of dependent var   3033848.
Adjusted R-squared    0.781882   S.D. of dependent var   127916.1
S.E. of regression    59740.84   Sum of squared resid    2.57D+11
Durbin-Watson stat    0.637461   F-statistic             133.6328
Log likelihood       -929.7224
=====================================================================
```

>_COVA NTO1 RGNP(-1) RTTO(-1)_

SMPL 1965.2 - 1983.4
75 Observations
===

Series	Mean	S.D.	Maximum	Minimum
===
NTO1	3033848.0	127916.15	3257800.0	2681400.0
RGNP(-1)	1247.9658	191.88148	1553.4100	906.60160
RTTO(-1)	421.37952	83.434595	541.90590	264.74180
===

	Covariance	Correlation
===
NTO1,NTO1	1.614D+10	1.0000000
NTO1,RGNP(-1)	21193573.	0.8751355
NTO1,RTTO(-1)	9338476.6	0.8868171
RGNP(-1),RGNP(-1)	36327.588	1.0000000
RGNP(-1),RTTO(-1)	15670.005	0.9920178
RTTO(-1),RTTO(-1)	6868.5139	1.0000000
===

>_LS NTO1 C RGNP(-1)_

SMPL 1965.2 - 1983.4
75 Observations
LS // Dependent Variable is NTO1
===

VARIABLE	COEFFICIENT	STD. ERROR	T-STAT.	2-TAIL SIG.
===
| C | 2305782.7 | 47662.445 | 48.377349 | 0.000 |
| RGNP(-1) | 583.40160 | 37.754326 | 15.452576 | 0.000 |
===

R-squared	0.765862	Mean of dependent var	3033848.
Adjusted R-squared	0.762655	S.D. of dependent var	127916.1
S.E. of regression	62318.31	Sum of squared resid	2.84D+11
Durbin-Watson stat	0.563561	F-statistic	238.7821
Log likelihood	-933.4076		
===

>_LS NTO1 C RTTO(-1)_

```
SMPL  1965.2 - 1983.4
75 Observations
LS // Dependent Variable is NTO1
=====================================================================
       VARIABLE    COEFFICIENT   STD. ERROR    T-STAT.   2-TAIL SIG.
=====================================================================
          C        2460937.6     35611.314    69.105500    0.000
       RTTO(-1)    1359.6066     82.922644    16.396083    0.000
=====================================================================
R-squared              0.786445   Mean of dependent var    3033848.
Adjusted R-squared     0.783519   S.D. of dependent var    127916.1
S.E. of regression     59516.20   Sum of squared resid     2.59D+11
Durbin-Watson stat     0.622562   F-statistic              268.8315
Log likelihood         -929.9571
=====================================================================
```

The statistical results clearly point to the possibility of multicollinearity. The correlation coefficient of RGNP(-1) and RTTO(-1) is higher than either of the r values that measure the correlation between each of the explanatory variables and the dependent variables.   Also, the measured t statistics increased when one of the explanatory variables was dropped.

5.1-10.   >*FETCH NTO1 CUN INR IRE GDE EXT IMP PDE*
           >*GENR RGDE=GDE/PDE*
           >*GENR RCUN=CUN/PDE*
           >*GENR RITO=(INR+IRE)/PDE*
           >*GENR RBAL=(EXT-IMP)/PDE*
           >*SMPL 65.2 83.4*
           >*LS NTO1 C RCUN(-1) RITO(-1) RGDE(-1) RBAL(-1)*

```
SMPL  1965.2 - 1983.4
75 Observations
LS // Dependent Variable is NTO1
=====================================================================
       VARIABLE    COEFFICIENT   STD. ERROR    T-STAT.   2-TAIL SIG.
=====================================================================
          C        2111035.1     77159.186    27.359478    0.000
       RCUN(-1)    34.078860     144.96297     0.2350867    0.815
       RITO(-1)    3320.5100     551.45658     6.0213445    0.000
       RGDE(-1)    3451.4905     780.42561     4.4225746    0.000
       RBAL(-1)    1239.2304     1008.7120     1.2285275    0.224
=====================================================================
R-squared              0.824990   Mean of dependent var    3033848.
Adjusted R-squared     0.814989   S.D. of dependent var    127916.1
S.E. of regression     55020.41   Sum of squared resid     2.12D+11
Durbin-Watson stat     0.793983   F-statistic              82.49419
Log likelihood         -922.4926
=====================================================================
```

>*COVA NTO1 RCUN(-1) RITO(-1) RGDE(-1) RBAL(-1)*

SMPL 1965.2 - 1983.4
75 Observations

Series	Mean	S.D.	Maximum	Minimum
NTO1	3033848.0	127916.15	3257800.0	2681400.0
RCUN(-1)	781.31035	128.98608	1007.7160	566.49040
RITO(-1)	188.27414	35.545065	254.48160	134.47200
RGDE(-1)	75.725322	9.7582949	93.985880	63.747140
RBAL(-1)	7.7914123	6.8500670	22.902600	-8.4549940

	Covariance	Correlation
NTO1,NTO1	1.614D+10	1.0000000
NTO1,RCUN(-1)	13858825.	0.8513100
NTO1,RITO(-1)	3918891.3	0.8735506
NTO1,RGDE(-1)	-13419.512	-0.0108960
NTO1,RBAL(-1)	-96632.004	-0.1117713
RCUN(-1),RCUN(-1)	16415.576	1.0000000
RCUN(-1),RITO(-1)	4187.1911	0.9256146
RCUN(-1),RGDE(-1)	-152.12050	-0.1224900
RCUN(-1),RBAL(-1)	-63.883545	-0.0732792
RITO(-1),RITO(-1)	1246.6056	1.0000000
RITO(-1),RGDE(-1)	-94.472548	-0.2760463
RITO(-1),RBAL(-1)	-29.936882	-0.1246126
RGDE(-1),RGDE(-1)	93.954662	1.0000000
RGDE(-1),RBAL(-1)	-15.188457	-0.2302897
RBAL(-1),RBAL(-1)	46.297772	1.0000000

Multicollinearity appears to be present. RCUN(-1) and RITO(-1) have high standard deviations and very low measured t statistics. The examination of the correlation coefficients, however, is not sufficient to detect the presence of multicollinearity since a simple correlation coefficient, r, cannot account for all of the complex relationships between variables.

5.1-11. Fetch and generate all necessary variables. After all the generations are completed, delete all unnecessary variables and save the work file as WF5-1-11.

>*FETCH NCN1 NMN1 NWR1 NSR1 INR IRE GDE PDE EXT IMP CUN*
>*GENR ITO=INR+IRE*
>*GENR RITO=ITO/PDE*
>*GENR RGDE=GDE/PDE*
>*GENR BAL=EXT-IMP*

>*GENR RBAL=BAL/PDE*
>*GENR RCUN=CUN/PDE*
>*D IRE GDE PDE EXT IMP BAL CUN ITO*
>*SAVE WF5-1-11*

>*EDIT BA5-1-11*

```
1:  LOAD WF5-1-11
2:  SMPL 65.2 83.4
3:  LS(P) NCN1 C RCUN(-1) RITO(-1) RGDE(-1) RBAL(-1)
4:  LS(P) NMN1 C RCUN(-1) RITO(-1) RGDE(-1) RBAL(-1)
5:  LS(P) NWR1 C RCUN(-1) RITO(-1) RGDE(-1) RBAL(-1)
6:  LS(P) NSR1 C RCUN(-1) RITO(-1) RGDE(-1) RBAL(-1)
7:  .X BA5-1-11
```

>*RUN BA5-1-11*

```
SMPL  1965.2 - 1983.4
75 Observations
LS // Dependent Variable is NCN1
======================================================================
        VARIABLE   COEFFICIENT   STD. ERROR      T-STAT.   2-TAIL SIG.
======================================================================
           C        116364.51    15391.584     7.5602689     0.000
        RCUN(-1)   -138.32625    28.916967    -4.7835668     0.000
        RITO(-1)    450.30798    110.00363     4.0935740     0.000
        RGDE(-1)    303.10409    155.67798     1.9469940     0.056
        RBAL(-1)   -179.73316    201.21617    -0.8932342     0.375
======================================================================
R-squared              0.288846   Mean of dependent var    114622.4
Adjusted R-squared     0.248209   S.D. of dependent var    12658.17
S.E. of regression     10975.38   Sum of squared resid     8.43D+09
Durbin-Watson stat     1.505026   F-statistic              7.107900
Log likelihood        -801.5889
======================================================================
```

81

```
SMPL   1965.2 - 1983.4
75 Observations
LS // Dependent Variable is NMN1
=================================================================
    VARIABLE    COEFFICIENT    STD. ERROR      T-STAT.   2-TAIL SIG.
=================================================================
        C        1209310.8     37194.634     32.513045    0.000
    RCUN(-1)    -1368.7161     69.879488    -19.586808    0.000
    RITO(-1)     3035.5041    265.82999      11.418968    0.000
    RGDE(-1)     1996.0576    376.20465       5.3057759   0.000
    RBAL(-1)      491.53494   486.25025       1.0108683   0.316
=================================================================
R-squared              0.919353   Mean of dependent var    866407.5
Adjusted R-squared     0.914745   S.D. of dependent var    90835.72
S.E. of regression     26522.62   Sum of squared resid     4.92D+10
Durbin-Watson stat     0.529994   F-statistic              199.4962
Log likelihood        -867.7647
=================================================================


SMPL   1965.2 - 1983.4
75 Observations
LS // Dependent Variable is NWR1
=================================================================
    VARIABLE    COEFFICIENT    STD. ERROR      T-STAT.   2-TAIL SIG.
=================================================================
        C        341725.39     20637.868     16.558173    0.000
    RCUN(-1)      297.64679     38.773433     7.6765653    0.000
    RITO(-1)      406.59774    147.49881      2.7566171    0.008
    RGDE(-1)      553.22959    208.74145      2.6503102    0.010
    RBAL(-1)      208.57701    269.80151      0.7730758    0.442
=================================================================
R-squared              0.927750   Mean of dependent var    694350.3
Adjusted R-squared     0.923621   S.D. of dependent var    53249.32
S.E. of regression     14716.38   Sum of squared resid     1.52D+10
Durbin-Watson stat     1.399368   F-statistic              224.7132
Log likelihood        -823.5869
=================================================================
```

```
SMPL   1965.2 - 1983.4
75 Observations
LS // Dependent Variable is NSR1
========================================================================
        VARIABLE    COEFFICIENT   STD. ERROR    T-STAT.   2-TAIL SIG.
========================================================================
           C        -60097.553    16155.186   -3.7200162    0.000
        RCUN(-1)     804.36529     30.351586   26.501590     0.000
        RITO(-1)    -469.69804    115.46109    -4.0680202    0.000
        RGDE(-1)    1207.9362     163.40142     7.3924462    0.000
        RBAL(-1)     538.47934    211.19883     2.5496322    0.013
------------------------------------------------------------------------
R-squared               0.984035   Mean of dependent var    575596.3
Adjusted R-squared      0.983122   S.D. of dependent var    88672.96
S.E. of regression     11519.89    Sum of squared resid     9.29D+09
Durbin-Watson stat      0.971532   F-statistic              1078.619
Log likelihood          -805.2204
========================================================================
```

Study Project:

5.1-12.

y_t	x_{1t}	x_{2t}	$x_{1t}y_t$	x_{1t}^2	$x_{1t}x_{2t}$	$x_{2t}y_t$	x_{2t}^2
7.4	8.0	4.0	59.2	64.0	32.0	29.6	16.0
9.8	11.0	5.5	107.8	121.0	60.5	53.9	30.25
8.0	9.0	4.5	72.0	81.0	40.5	36.0	20.25
5.3	6.0	3.0	31.8	36.0	18.0	15.9	7.0
5.7	6.0	3.0	34.2	36.0	18.0	17.1	9.0
$\Sigma=36.2$	$\Sigma=40.0$	$\Sigma=20.0$	$\Sigma=305.0$	$\Sigma=338.0$	$\Sigma=169.0$	$\Sigma=152.5$	$\Sigma=84.5$

E1: $36.2 = 5.0\ \hat{b}_0 + 40.0\ \hat{b}_1 + 20.0\ \hat{b}_2$

E2: $305.0 = 40.0\ \hat{b}_0 + 338.0\ \hat{b}_1 + 169.0\ \hat{b}_2$

E3: $152.5 = 20.0\ \hat{b}_0 + 169.0\ \hat{b}_1 + 84.5\ \hat{b}_2$

Using Cramers Rule and solving with matrix algebra:

$$\hat{b}_0 = \frac{\begin{vmatrix} 36.2 & 40.0 & 20.0 \\ 305.0 & 338.0 & 169.0 \\ 314.1 & 169.0 & 84.5 \end{vmatrix}}{|A|}$$

83

But the determinant of A is

$$|A| = \begin{vmatrix} 5.0 & 40.0 & 20.0 & 5.0 & 40.0 \\ 40.0 & 338.0 & 169.0 & 40.0 & 338.0 \\ 20.0 & 169.0 & 84.5 & 20.0 & 169.0 \end{vmatrix}$$

and $|A| = 142,805 + 135,200 + 135,200 - 135,200 - 142,805 - 135,200 = 0$

Since $|A| = 0$ a singular matrix results and it is impossible to solve for $\hat{b}_0$. Since $|A|$ is also the denominator in solving for $\hat{b}_1$ and $\hat{b}_2$, these parameter estimates cannot be derived.

5.2 Exercises

Questions for Review:

5.2-1.   Autocorrelation can occur because of random shocks which are not explained by the independent variables in a regression equation. In addition, autocorrelation can result from specification errors such as missing variables and incorrect functional form.

5.2-2.   It is necessary to arrange the cross-section observations in some logical order of magnitude so that the presence of autocorrelation can be examined. Usually, the dependent variable is placed in rank order.

For example, a cross-section study might involve explaining the gross state product for twenty-five states on the basis of each state's tax rate and population. In order to examine the presence of autocorrelation, the states should be ranked from high-to-low on the basis of gross state product before analyzing the residuals.

5.2-3.

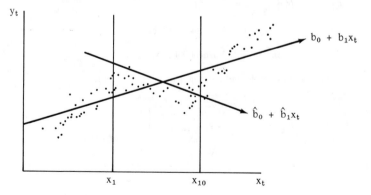

Although $\hat{b}_1$ is an unbiased estimator of b_1, the estimated regression line over the sample period fits the data more closely than the true line. Hence, s_e and $s_{\hat{b}_1}$ are downward biased, and the t_m statistics are upward biased.

5.2-4.   Another strategy that might work is to improve the specification of an equation by adding missing explanatory variables or finding a more appropriate functional form.

5.2-5.   From Exercise 5.2-7.

NTO1 = 2,357,473.6 + 548.04637 RGNP(-1)

RHO = .674

Given:

	RGNP	NTO1
83:2	1,525.052	3,155,600
83:3	1,553.409	3,213,100
83:4	1,571.912	3,227,500

$$\widehat{NTO1}_{83:4} = \hat{\rho}(\widehat{NTO1}_{83:3}) + \hat{b}_0(1 - \hat{\rho})$$

$$+ \hat{b}_1(RGNP_{83:3} - \hat{\rho}(RGNP_{83:2}))$$

$$= .674(3,213,000) + 2,357,473.6(1 - .674)$$

$$+ 548.046(1,553.409 - .674(1,525.052))$$

$$= 2,165,562 + 768,536.39 + 548.046(525.529)$$

$$= 2,165,562 + 768,536.39 + 288,014.07$$

$$= 3,222,112.46$$

$$\widehat{NTO1}_{84:1} = \hat{\rho}(\widehat{NTO1}_{83:4}) + \hat{b}_0(1 - \hat{\rho})$$

$$+ \hat{b}_1(RGNP_{83:4} - \hat{\rho}(RGNP_{83:3}))$$

$$= .674(3,227,500) + 2,357,473.6(1 - .674)$$

$$+ 548.046(1,571.912 - .674(1,553.409))$$

$$= 2,175,335 + 768,536.40 + 548.046(524.912)$$

$$= 2,175,335 + 768,536.40 + 287,675.92$$

$$= 3,231,547.32$$

5.2-6.

$$H_0: \rho \leq 0$$
$$H_1: \rho > 0$$

From Computer Session 5.2-3, $DW_m = 1.25$.

At a 0.05 level of significance, 74 observations, and k = 4, $DW_{c,l} = 1.51$ and $DW_{c,u} = 1.74$.

Since 1.24 < 1.51, reject H_0 and accept H_1. It is concluded, therefore, that $\hat{\rho}$ is significantly different from zero (i.e., positive autocorrelation is present).

Computer Exercises:

5.2-7.   >*FETCH NTO1 GNP PDE*
             >*GENR RGNP=GNP/PDE*
             >*SMPL 65.2 83.4*
             >*LS NTO1 C RGNP(-1)*

```
SMPL  1965.2 - 1983.4
75 Observations
LS // Dependent Variable is NTO1
================================================================
        VARIABLE   COEFFICIENT   STD. ERROR    T-STAT.   2-TAIL SIG.
================================================================
           C       2305782.7    47662.445    48.377349    0.000
        RGNP(-1)   583.40160    37.754326    15.452576    0.000
================================================================
R-squared            0.765862   Mean of dependent var   3033848.
Adjusted R-squared   0.762655   S.D. of dependent var   127916.1
S.E. of regression   62318.31   Sum of squared resid    2.84D+11
Durbin-Watson stat   0.563561   F-statistic             238.7821
Log likelihood      -933.4076
================================================================
                      Covariance Matrix
================================================================
C,C                  2.27D+09   C,RGNP(-1)              -1778837.
RGNP(-1),RGNP(-1)    1425.389
================================================================
================================================================
          Residual Plot          obs RESIDUAL  ACTUAL   FITTED
================================================================
|  *      :   |   :     | 65.2 -153296.  2681400  2834696
|     *   :   |   :     | 65.3 -114179.  2728100  2842279
|        *:   |   :     | 65.4 -68787.4  2781900  2850687
```

```
|    *    :    |    :    | 66.1 -125268.  2738700  2863968
|        :*    |    :    | 66.2 -54551.7  2820300  2874852
|        :   *|    :    | 66.3 -6447.60  2870700  2877148
|        :    | *  :    | 66.4  40562.9  2922700  2882137
|        : *  |    :    | 67.1 -35833.5  2851400  2887233
|        :    |*   :    | 67.2  11857.6  2899700  2887842
|        :    |  *:    | 67.3  54864.2  2946500  2891636
|        :    |  *    | 67.4  64023.1  2962700  2898677
|        :   *|    :    | 68.1  698.386  2905900  2905202
|        :    |  *:    | 68.2  51663.7  2962200  2910536
|        :    |  :*    | 68.3  67885.7  2989600  2921714
|        :    |  :  *   | 68.4  88225.3  3017200  2928975
|        :    | *  :    | 69.1  35461.5  2966600  2931138
|        :    |  : *   | 69.2  86624.2  3024900  2938276
|        :    |  :    * | 69.3  116948.  3057900  2940952
|        :    |  :    * | 69.4  115003.  3057800  2942797
|        :    | *  :    | 70.1  42814.9  2981900  2939085
|        :    | *  :    | 70.2  39872.3  2976500  2936628
|        :    |  :*    | 70.3  67385.8  3005000  2937614
|        :    | *  :    | 70.4  43446.4  2987100  2943654
|        : *  |    :    | 71.1 -39537.8  2899000  2938538
|        :   *|    :    | 71.2 -8361.04  2945900  2954261
|        :    |*   :    | 71.3  11599.7  2969000  2957400
|        :   *|    :    | 71.4 -62.8384  2962500  2962563
|       *:    |    :    | 72.1 -68497.4  2899700  2968197
|        : *  |    :    | 72.2 -20502.1  2960400  2980902
|        :   *|    :    | 72.3 -2642.54  2990700  2993343
|        :   *|    :    | 72.4 -7949.08  2993900  3001849
|       *     |    :    | 73.1 -60994.3  2953500  3014494
|        :    |*   :    | 73.2  8277.62  3041400  3033122
|        :    |  *:    | 73.3  47054.1  3081100  3034046
|        :    |  :*    | 73.4  70638.1  3109000  3038362
|        :    |*   :    | 74.1  12303.4  3056700  3044397
|        :    |  :*    | 74.2  72515.5  3109500  3036985
|        :    |  :  *   | 74.3  88340.2  3126100  3037760
|        :    |  :  *   | 74.4  84394.2  3117600  3033206
|        : *  |    :    | 75.1 -42153.4  2981400  3023553
|        : *  |    :    | 75.2 -37852.3  2970500  3008352
|        : *  |    :    | 75.3 -43844.3  2973000  3016844
|        : *  |    :    | 75.4 -45032.1  2987700  3032732
|     *   :    |    :    | 76.1 -107398.  2931900  3039298
|       *:    |    :    | 76.2 -67535.1  2987900  3055435
|        :   *|    :    | 76.3 -11517.1  3049000  3060517
|        :   *|    :    | 76.4 -19332.6  3045500  3064833
|     *   :    |    :    | 77.1 -111108.  2960500  3071608
|        :   *|    :    | 77.2 -24657.3  3063600  3088257
|        :   *|    :    | 77.3 -18724.2  3082400  3101124
```

87

```
|        :     *     :      | 77.4   1237.01  3115500  3114263
|        :*    |     :      | 78.1  -52741.1  3063100  3115841
|        :     |*    :      | 78.2   6946.82  3129500  3122553
|        :     |   * :      | 78.3   37088.4  3181200  3144112
|        :     |   * :      | 78.4   32771.6  3183800  3151028
|        :   * |     :      | 79.1  -19149.7  3143300  3162450
|        :     |  *:        | 79.2   47515.8  3212400  3164884
|        :     |   : *      | 79.3   78983.6  3241900  3162916
|        :     |   : *      | 79.4   84688.1  3257800  3173112
|        :     |*   :       | 80.1   20811.7  3195500  3174688
|        :     |  *:        | 80.2   50018.6  3228800  3178781
|        :     |   :*       | 80.3   75429.5  3233800  3158370
|        :     |     *      | 80.4   63592.5  3223600  3160008
|        :     *     :      | 81.1   1919.69  3169900  3167980
|        :    |*    :       | 81.2   5629.49  3192400  3186771
|        :   *|     :       | 81.3  -6087.00  3182100  3188187
|        :  * |     :       | 81.4  -26234.0  3169700  3195934
|     *  :    |     :       | 82.1  -90415.3  3094500  3184915
|      *:     |     :       | 82.2  -74765.8  3097800  3172566
|     *  :    |     :       | 82.3  -89245.1  3085400  3174645
|  *     :    |     :       | 82.4  -128442.  3044100  3172542
|        *    |     :       | 83.1  -59361.6  3110300  3169662
|        :  * |     :       | 83.2  -19542.1  3155600  3175142
|        :    |*    :       | 83.3   17499.5  3213000  3195501
|        :    |*   :        | 83.4   15455.4  3227500  3212045
===================================================================
```

>*SMPL 65.3 83.4*
>*LS NTO1 C RGNP(-1) AR(1)*

```
SMPL   1965.3 - 1983.4
74 Observations
LS // Dependent Variable is NTO1
Convergence achieved after 1 iterations
===================================================================
       VARIABLE    COEFFICIENT    STD. ERROR     T-STAT.    2-TAIL SIG.
===================================================================
          C        2357473.6      103095.85    22.866815      0.000
       RGNP(-1)    548.04637      80.255232     6.8287931     0.000
-------------------------------------------------------------------
       AR(1)       0.6739675      0.0801162     8.4123748     0.000
===================================================================
R-squared              0.880644    Mean of dependent var    3038611.
Adjusted R-squared     0.877282    S.D. of dependent var    121910.0
S.E. of regression     42706.40    Sum of squared resid     1.29D+11
Durbin-Watson stat     2.045784    F-statistic              261.9306
Log likelihood         -892.4659
```

88

```
==================================================================
                      Covariance Matrix
==================================================================
C,C                      1.06D+10   C,RGNP(-1)            -8183716.
C,AR(1)                  80.51134   RGNP(-1),RGNP(-1)     6440.902
RGNP(-1),AR(1)          -0.025407   AR(1),AR(1)           0.006419
==================================================================
```

```
==================================================================
            Residual Plot                 obs RESIDUAL  ACTUAL  FITTED
==================================================================
|          :    *  |    :        | 65.3 -16806.0 2728100 2744906
|          :     * |    :        | 65.4  2422.62 2781900 2779477
|     *    :       |    :        | 66.1 -84189.3 2738700 2822889
|          :       | *  :        | 66.2  24710.2 2820300 2795590
|          :       | * :         | 66.3  24848.5 2870700 2845852
|          :       |  *          | 66.4  39646.9 2922700 2883053
|       *  :       |    :        | 67.1 -68327.9 2851400 2919728
|          :       |  *:         | 67.2  30680.6 2899700 2869019
|          :       |  *          | 67.3  41749.9 2946500 2904750
|          :       | *  :        | 67.4  22195.6 2962700 2940504
|         *:       |    :        | 68.1 -47194.1 2905900 2953094
|          :       |    :*       | 68.2  46506.9 2962200 2915693
|          :       | *  :        | 68.3  28839.4 2989600 2960761
|          :       |  *          | 68.4  38229.3 3017200 2978971
|          : *     |    :        | 69.1 -28408.1 2966600 2995008
|          :       |    : *      | 69.2  58659.8 3024900 2966240
|          :       |    : *      | 69.3  54372.4 3057900 3003528
|          :       |  *:         | 69.4  31992.8 3057800 3025807
|          *       |    :        | 70.1 -39185.2 2981900 3021085
|          :       |* :          | 70.2  6527.46 2976500 2969973
|          :       |  *:         | 70.3  36184.4 3005000 2968816
|          :    *  |    :        | 70.4 -5972.51 2987100 2993073
|     *    :       |    :        | 71.1 -73379.0 2899000 2972379
|          :       |  * :        | 71.2  14888.2 2945900 2931012
|          :       |  * :        | 71.3  13384.9 2969000 2955615
|          :    *  |    :        | 71.4 -11545.9 2962500 2974046
|     *    :       |    :        | 72.1 -71989.7 2899700 2971690
|          :       | *  :        | 72.2  22668.0 2960400 2937732
|          :       |*  :         | 72.3  8415.35 2990700 2982285
|          :     * |    :        | 72.4 -8920.55 2993900 3002821
|        * :       |    :        | 73.1 -57970.5 2953500 3011470
|          :       |    :*       | 73.2  47664.7 3041400 2993735
|          :       |    *        | 73.3  39049.2 3081100 3042051
|          :       |  *:         | 73.4  36723.0 3109000 3072277
|          :*      |    :        | 74.1 -37317.1 3056700 3094017
|          :       |    :  *     | 74.2  61515.0 3109500 3047985
```

89

```
|          :    |   *:      | 74.3   37108.4   3126100   3088992
|          :    | *   :     | 74.4   22189.5   3117600   3095411
|   *      :    |    :       | 75.1  -102098.   2981400   3083498
|          :  * |    :       | 75.2  -13034.6   2970500   2983535
|          : *  |    :       | 75.3  -20789.8   2973000   2993790
|          : *  |    :       | 75.4  -17323.2   2987700   3005023
|      *   :    |    :       | 76.1  -79139.3   2931900   3011039
|          :    |*   :       | 76.2   3465.38   2987900   2984435
|          :    |   *:       | 76.3   32266.2   3049000   3016734
|          :  * |    :       | 76.4  -13249.6   3045500   3058750
|   *      :    |    :       | 77.1  -99523.5   2960500   3060023
|          :    |   :*       | 77.2   49513.4   3063600   3014087
|          :   *|    :       | 77.3  -2718.84   3082400   3085119
|          :    | * :        | 77.4   13514.4   3115500   3101986
|        * :    |    :       | 78.1  -54358.0   3063100   3117458
|          :    |    *       | 78.2   42051.8   3129500   3087448
|          :    |   *:       | 78.3   32997.9   3181200   3148202
|          :    |*   :       | 78.4   7905.35   3183800   3175895
|          :  * |    :       | 79.1  -40696.9   3143300   3183997
|          :    |    :  *     | 79.2   60642.9   3212400   3151757
|          :    |   :*        | 79.3   46961.7   3241900   3194938
|          :    |   *:        | 79.4   32156.0   3257800   3225644
|        :*     |    :        | 80.1  -35885.8   3195500   3231386
|          :    |   *:        | 80.2   36555.3   3228800   3192245
|          :    |    *        | 80.3   40877.6   3233800   3192922
|          :    | * :         | 80.4   12847.3   3223600   3210753
|          :  * |    :        | 81.1  -40431.4   3169900   3210331
|          :    |*   :        | 81.2   5656.96   3192400   3186743
|          :   *|    :        | 81.3  -9241.43   3182100   3191341
|          : *  |    :        | 81.4  -21080.3   3169700   3190780
|      *   :    |    :        | 82.1  -72667.3   3094500   3167167
|          : *  |    :        | 82.2  -14060.1   3097800   3111860
|       *  :    |    :        | 82.3  -38456.2   3085400   3123856
|     *    :    |    :        | 82.4  -68106.9   3044100   3112207
|          :    | * :         | 83.1   27302.2   3110300   3082998
|          :    | * :         | 83.2   21013.6   3155600   3134586
|          :    |  *:         | 83.3   32228.1   3213000   3180772
|          :    |*   :        | 83.4   5390.18   3227500   3222110
=====================================================================
```

As shown, the Durbin Watson statistic is 0.563 for the OLSQ run and it
increases to 2.045 when the CORC-adjustment is made. Hence the OLSQ
operation indicates the presence of positive autocorrelation (reject H_0),
while the CORC-adjusted equation shows no positive autocorrelation
(cannot reject H_0).

The residual plots suggest that the CORC-adjusted equation has more
randomly distributed errors than the OLSQ equation.

90

5.2-8.   After generating and estimating the CORC-adjusted regression equation, expand the sample period to 84.4 and forecast CONTO1.

>*FETCH NTO1 GNP PDE*
>*SMPL 65.1 83.4*
>*GENR RGNP=GNP/PDE*
>*SMPL 65.3 83.4*
>*LS NTO1 C RGNP(-1) AR(1)*

```
SMPL   1965.3 - 1983.4
74 Observations
LS // Dependent Variable is NTO1
Convergence achieved after 1 iterations
=======================================================================
        VARIABLE    COEFFICIENT   STD. ERROR    T-STAT.    2-TAIL SIG.
=======================================================================
          C         2357473.6     103095.85    22.866815    0.000
       RGNP(-1)     548.04637     80.255232     6.8287931    0.000
- - - - - - - - - - - - - - - - - - - - - - - - - - - - - - - - - - - -
        AR(1)       0.6739675     0.0801162     8.4123748    0.000
=======================================================================
R-squared             0.880644   Mean of dependent var   3038611.
Adjusted R-squared    0.877282   S.D. of dependent var   121910.0
S.E. of regression    42706.40   Sum of squared resid    1.29D+11
Durbin-Watson stat    2.045784   F-statistic             261.9306
Log likelihood       -892.4659
=======================================================================
```

>*EXPAND 65.1 84.4*
>*DATA RGNP*

OBS.	RGNP
1965.1	*N84.1*
1984.1	*1595*
1984.2	*1601*
1984.3	*1616*
1984.4	*END*

>*SMPL 84.1 84.4*
>*FORCST CONTO1*
>*PRINT CONTO1*

91

```
====================
  obs      CONTO1
====================
1984.1    3231548.
1984.2    3240095.
1984.3    3240616.
1984.4    3246972.
====================
```

Manually:

$$\widehat{NTO1}_{84:1} = .674(3,227,500) + 2,357,473.6(1 - .674)$$

$$+ 548.046(1,571.912 - .674(1,553.409))$$

$$= 3,231,547.32$$

The manual computation of 3,231,547.32 for NTO1 in 84:1 is the same as the computer generated forecast after allowing for rounding error.

5.2-9.   >*FETCH CUN DSY PRR*
              >*LS CUN C DSY PRR*

```
SMPL  1965.1 - 1983.4
76 Observations
LS // Dependent Variable is CUN
=========================================================================
        VARIABLE    COEFFICIENT   STD. ERROR    T-STAT.   2-TAIL SIG.
=========================================================================
           C        -10.983681    3.2859794   -3.3425896    0.001
          DSY         0.9336403   0.0037433   249.41440     0.000
          PRR        -2.0888293   0.5530677    -3.7768058    0.000
=========================================================================
R-squared               0.999566   Mean of dependent var   1054.113
Adjusted R-squared      0.999554   S.D. of dependent var    542.6438
S.E. of regression     11.46367    Sum of squared resid    9593.347
Durbin-Watson stat      0.850483   F-statistic             83989.50
Log likelihood       -291.6868
=========================================================================
```

>*SMPL 65.2 83.4*
>*LS CUN C DSY PRR AR(1)*

```
SMPL  1965.2 - 1983.4
75 Observations
LS // Dependent Variable is CUN
Convergence achieved after 2 iterations
===================================================================
    VARIABLE   COEFFICIENT  STD. ERROR    T-STAT.   2-TAIL SIG.
===================================================================
       C       -14.311000   6.6213286   -2.1613486    0.034
      DSY       0.9283033   0.0060285  153.98511       0.000
      PRR      -1.0636805   0.7827666   -1.3588731     0.179
-------------------------------------------------------------------
     AR(1)      0.6061823   0.0936313    6.4741430     0.000
===================================================================
R-squared            0.999712   Mean of dependent var   1062.596
Adjusted R-squared   0.999700   S.D. of dependent var    541.2012
S.E. of regression   9.374077   Sum of squared resid    6239.005
Durbin-Watson stat   2.022470   F-statistic            82195.11
Log likelihood    -272.2112
===================================================================
```

The CORC adjustment caused some reduction in the value of the measured t statistics. The DW statistic, however, increased to 2.02, thus showing no significant presence of positive autocorrelation.

5.2-10.   >*LOAD WF4-4-7*
>*SMPL 65.2 83.4*
>*LS NCN C BTO(-1)*

```
SMPL  1965.2 - 1983.4
75 Observations
LS // Dependent Variable is NCN
===================================================================
    VARIABLE   COEFFICIENT  STD. ERROR    T-STAT.   2-TAIL SIG.
===================================================================
       C       15002.036    1464.1964   10.245918     0.000
   BTO(-1)      0.0567081   0.0049704   11.409144     0.000
===================================================================
R-squared            0.640692   Mean of dependent var   30032.51
Adjusted R-squared   0.635770   S.D. of dependent var    9169.378
S.E. of regression   5533.851   Sum of squared resid    2.24D+09
Durbin-Watson stat   0.790726   F-statistic             130.1686
Log likelihood    -751.8048
===================================================================
```

>*LS NCN1 C BTO1(-1)*

SMPL   1965.2 - 1983.4
75 Observations
LS // Dependent Variable is NCN1
==

VARIABLE	COEFFICIENT	STD. ERROR	T-STAT.	2-TAIL SIG.

==

C	112895.22	3991.2514	28.285669	0.000
BTO1(-1)	0.0097256	0.0208955	0.4654380	0.643

==

R-squared	0.002959	Mean of dependent var	114622.4
Adjusted R-squared	-0.010699	S.D. of dependent var	12658.17
S.E. of regression	12725.71	Sum of squared resid	1.18D+10
Durbin-Watson stat	1.030332	F-statistic	0.216633
Log likelihood	-814.2603		

==

>*SMPL 66.2 83.4*
>*LS PRR C PRMNS(-1)*

SMPL   1966.2 - 1983.4
71 Observations
LS // Dependent Variable is PRR
==

VARIABLE	COEFFICIENT	STD. ERROR	T-STAT.	2-TAIL SIG.

==

C	9.4336488	0.4480904	21.053006	0.000
PRMNS(-1)	-0.4625166	0.1611000	-2.8709903	0.006

==

R-squared	0.106710	Mean of dependent var	9.291718
Adjusted R-squared	0.093764	S.D. of dependent var	3.941984
S.E. of regression	3.752628	Sum of squared resid	971.6728
Durbin-Watson stat	0.192943	F-statistic	8.242585
Log likelihood	-193.6247		

==

>*SMPL 67.1 83.4*
>*LS PRR C PRMNS(-4)*

```
SMPL  1967.1 - 1983.4
68 Observations
LS // Dependent Variable is PRR
====================================================================
     VARIABLE   COEFFICIENT  STD. ERROR    T-STAT.   2-TAIL SIG.
====================================================================
        C        9.4533622   0.4699066   20.117536    0.000
    PRMNS(-4)   -0.3809821   0.1932315   -1.9716352   0.053
====================================================================
R-squared               0.055623   Mean of dependent var   9.446000
Adjusted R-squared      0.041314   S.D. of dependent var   3.957438
S.E. of regression      3.874827   Sum of squared resid    990.9425
Durbin-Watson stat      0.148624   F-statistic             3.887345
Log likelihood       -187.5789
====================================================================
```

>*SMPL 65.3 83.4*
>*LS NCN C BTO(-1) AR(1)*

```
SMPL  1965.3 - 1983.4
74 Observations
LS // Dependent Variable is NCN
Convergence achieved after 3 iterations
====================================================================
     VARIABLE   COEFFICIENT  STD. ERROR    T-STAT.   2-TAIL SIG.
====================================================================
        C        31728.550   7642.2875   4.1517085    0.000
    BTO(-1)      0.0080312   0.0026575   3.0220421    0.004
--------------------------------------------------------------------
    AR(1)        0.9653494   0.0285320   33.833973    0.000
====================================================================
R-squared               0.951430   Mean of dependent var   30149.70
Adjusted R-squared      0.950062   S.D. of dependent var   9175.239
S.E. of regression      2050.368   Sum of squared resid    2.98D+08
Durbin-Watson stat      1.820885   F-statistic             695.4105
Log likelihood       -667.7775
====================================================================
```

>*LS NCN1 C BTO1(-1) AR(1)*

```
SMPL  1965.3 - 1983.4
74 Observations
LS // Dependent Variable is NCN1
Convergence achieved after 3 iterations
=================================================================
        VARIABLE   COEFFICIENT   STD. ERROR    T-STAT.   2-TAIL SIG.
=================================================================
           C        114009.96    5136.6404    22.195433    0.000
        BTO1(-1)    0.0038941    0.0245769     0.1584464    0.875
-----------------------------------------------------------------
        AR(1)       0.4844080    0.1078339     4.4921672    0.000
=================================================================
R-squared              0.235272   Mean of dependent var    114713.3
Adjusted R-squared     0.213730   S.D. of dependent var    12719.94
S.E. of regression     11279.00   Sum of squared resid     9.03D+09
Durbin-Watson stat     1.799611   F-statistic              10.92172
Log likelihood        -793.9419
=================================================================
```

>*SMPL 66.3 83,4*
>*LS PRR C PRMNS(-1) AR(1)*

```
SMPL  1966.3 - 1983.4
70 Observations
LS // Dependent Variable is PRR
Convergence achieved after 2 iterations
=================================================================
        VARIABLE   COEFFICIENT   STD. ERROR    T-STAT.   2-TAIL SIG.
=================================================================
           C        10.314622    2.9494440     3.4971412    0.001
        PRMNS(-1)   0.2334855    0.1058862     2.2050611    0.031
-----------------------------------------------------------------
        AR(1)       0.9464817    0.0365146    25.920635     0.000
=================================================================
R-squared              0.898153   Mean of dependent var    9.345786
Adjusted R-squared     0.895113   S.D. of dependent var    3.943841
S.E. of regression     1.277262   Sum of squared resid     109.3036
Durbin-Watson stat     1.403661   F-statistic              295.4259
Log likelihood        -114.9229
=================================================================
```

>*SMPL 67.2 83.4*
>*LS PRR C PRMNS(-4) AR(1)*

```
SMPL  1967.2 - 1983.4
67 Observations
LS // Dependent Variable is PRR
Convergence achieved after 2 iterations
========================================================================
    VARIABLE    COEFFICIENT   STD. ERROR    T-STAT.    2-TAIL SIG.
========================================================================
        C        10.628104    2.7443143    3.8727722    0.000
    PRMNS(-4)     0.0484548   0.1173105    0.4130474    0.681
------------------------------------------------------------------------
     AR(1)        0.9371867   0.0418572   22.390079     0.000
========================================================================
R-squared              0.887362   Mean of dependent var    9.500313
Adjusted R-squared     0.883842   S.D. of dependent var    3.961688
S.E. of regression     1.350223   Sum of squared resid    116.6786
Durbin-Watson stat     1.727252   F-statistic             252.0948
Log likelihood      -113.6524
========================================================================
```

Critical t Values

Level of Significance	t_c
0.01	2.390
0.05	1.671
0.10	1.296

(a)

$$H_0: b_1 \leq 0$$
$$H_1: b_1 > 0$$

$t_m = 3.02$　　　　$n = 74$　　　　$df = 72$

Since t_m is greater than the critical t values at all three levels of significance, the null hypothesis is rejected. Therefore, it is concluded that lagged building valuation positively influences construction employment in Orange County.

(b)

$$H_0: b_1 \leq 0$$
$$H_1: b_1 > 0$$

$t_m = 0.158$　　　　$n = 74$　　　　$df = 72$

97

Since t_m is less than the critical t values at all three levels of significance, the null hypothesis is accepted. Therefore, it is appropriate to conclude that lagged building valuation in Chicago does not have a significant positive impact on Chicago's construction employment.

(c)

$$H_0: b_1 \geq 0$$
$$H_1: b_1 < 0$$

$$t_m = 2.205 \qquad n = 70 \qquad df = 68$$

Since t_m is greater than 1.671 and 1.296, the null hypothesis is rejected at 0.10 and 0.05 levels of significance, but it cannot be rejected at the 0.01 level. Therefore, it is appropriate to conclude that the annual percentage change in the real money supply in the prior quarter is expected to have a short-run impact of decreasing the nominal interest rate during the current quarter at a 0.05 level of significance.

(d)

$$H_0: b_1 = 0$$
$$H_1: b_1 \neq 0$$

$$t_m = 0.413 \qquad n = 67 \qquad df = 65$$

Since t_m is less than the critical t values at all three levels of significance, the null hypothesis cannot be rejected. Therefore, it is appropriate to conclude that the annual percentage change in the real money supply lagged four quarters does not significantly influence the current nominal prime interest rate.

5.2-11. Load the work file created in Exercise 5.1-11 and make certain that RCUN, RITO, RGDE, RBAL, NCN1, NMN1, NWR1 and NSR1 are included. Save the workfile as WF5-2-11.

>*LOAD WF5-1-11*
>*SAVE WF5-2-11*
>*EDIT BA5-2-11*

```
1:  LOAD WF5-2-11
2:  SMPL 65.3 83.4
3:  LS(P) NCN1 C RCUN(-1) RITO(-1) RGDE(-1) RBAL(-1) AR(1)
4:  LS(P) NMN1 C RCUN(-1) RITO(-1) RGDE(-1) RBAL(-1) AR(1)
5:  LS(P) NWR1 C RCUN(-1) RITO(-1) RGDE(-1) RBAL(-1) AR(1)
6:  LS(P) NSR1 C RCUN(-1) RITO(-1) RGDE(-1) RBAL(-1) AR(1)
7:  .X BA5-2-11
```

>*RUN BA5-2-11*

```
SMPL  1965.3 - 1983.4
74 Observations
LS // Dependent Variable is NCN1
Convergence achieved after 3 iterations
=======================================================================
      VARIABLE   COEFFICIENT  STD. ERROR     T-STAT.   2-TAIL SIG.
=======================================================================
            C     121846.29    20603.449    5.9138784     0.000
      RCUN(-1)   -133.55508    36.465565   -3.6624987     0.001
      RITO(-1)    422.50220   138.82522     3.0434109     0.003
      RGDE(-1)    247.58944   203.78668     1.2149442     0.229
      RBAL(-1)   -127.94543   239.43127    -0.5343722     0.595
- - - - - - - - - - - - - - - - - - - - - - - - - - - - - - - - - - - -
        AR(1)    0.2531861     0.1172392    2.1595699     0.035
=======================================================================
R-squared              0.336142    Mean of dependent var    114713.3
Adjusted R-squared     0.287329    S.D. of dependent var    12719.94
S.E. of regression     10738.15    Sum of squared resid     7.84D+09
Durbin-Watson stat     1.800677    F-statistic              6.886306
Log likelihood         -788.7081
=======================================================================


SMPL  1965.3 - 1983.4
74 Observations
LS // Dependent Variable is NMN1
Convergence achieved after 5 iterations
=======================================================================
      VARIABLE   COEFFICIENT  STD. ERROR     T-STAT.   2-TAIL SIG.
=======================================================================
            C     1352556.0    84862.835    15.938143     0.000
      RCUN(-1)   -1141.3848   118.79592    -9.6079455     0.000
      RITO(-1)    1981.2331   403.91876     4.9050287     0.000
      RGDE(-1)    473.43830   755.60570     0.6265679     0.533
      RBAL(-1)    156.97528   492.53144     0.3187112     0.751
- - - - - - - - - - - - - - - - - - - - - - - - - - - - - - - - - - - -
        AR(1)    0.7682737     0.0677448    11.340709     0.000
=======================================================================
R-squared              0.968165    Mean of dependent var    865787.3
Adjusted R-squared     0.965825    S.D. of dependent var    91295.76
S.E. of regression     16877.49    Sum of squared resid     1.94D+10
Durbin-Watson stat     1.642966    F-statistic              413.6071
Log likelihood         -822.1693
=======================================================================
```

```
SMPL  1965.3 - 1983.4
74 Observations
LS // Dependent Variable is NWR1
Convergence achieved after 2 iterations
=================================================================
    VARIABLE    COEFFICIENT    STD. ERROR      T-STAT.    2-TAIL SIG.
=================================================================
       C         358705.42     27550.267     13.020035      0.000
    RCUN(-1)     305.94123     48.613871      6.2932908      0.000
    RITO(-1)     343.90909     184.98278      1.8591411      0.068
    RGDE(-1)     411.53009     272.10860      1.5123744      0.135
    RBAL(-1)     166.95621     315.22146      0.5296474      0.598
. . . . . . . . . . . . . . . . . . . . . . . . . . . . . . . . .

    AR(1)        0.2815591     0.1130097      2.4914588      0.015
=================================================================
R-squared                  0.932450   Mean of dependent var   695948.3
Adjusted R-squared         0.927483   S.D. of dependent var   51770.59
S.E. of regression         13941.25   Sum of squared resid    1.32D+10
Durbin-Watson stat         2.234240   F-statistic             187.7334
Log likelihood             -808.0258
=================================================================
```

```
SMPL  1965.3 - 1983.4
74 Observations
LS // Dependent Variable is NSR1
Convergence achieved after 3 iterations
=================================================================
    VARIABLE    COEFFICIENT    STD. ERROR      T-STAT.    2-TAIL SIG.
=================================================================
       C        -74009.150     29181.041     -2.5362067      0.014
    RCUN(-1)     802.19134     47.898884     16.747600       0.000
    RITO(-1)    -409.62760     182.48001     -2.2447807      0.028
    RGDE(-1)     1287.9217     279.97375      4.6001517      0.000
    RBAL(-1)     287.27634     269.77162      1.0648872      0.291
. . . . . . . . . . . . . . . . . . . . . . . . . . . . . . . . .

    AR(1)        0.5234025     0.1148665      4.5566145      0.000
=================================================================
R-squared                  0.987797   Mean of dependent var   577493.5
Adjusted R-squared         0.986899   S.D. of dependent var   87732.21
S.E. of regression         10041.64   Sum of squared resid    6.86D+09
Durbin-Watson stat         1.614729   F-statistic             1100.852
Log likelihood             -783.7455
=================================================================
```

A Comparison of t_m Statistics in CORC and OLSQ Tests

Dependent Variable	Test	RCUN(-1)	RITO(-1)	RGDE(-1)	RBAL(-1)
NCN1	OLSQ	-4.78	4.09	*1.94*	-0.89
	CORC	-3.66	3.04	1.21	-0.53
NMN1	OLSQ	-19.59	11.42	*5.30*	1.01
	CORC	-9.61	4.90	0.63	0.32
NWR1	OLSQ	2.68	2.76	2.65	0.77
	CORC	6.30	1.86	1.51	0.53
NSR1	OLSQ	26.50	-4.07	7.39	*2.54*
	CORC	16.75	-2.24	4.60	1.06

The values shown in italics are those which are not significant in the CORC-adjusted equation, but are significant in the OLSQ equation.

5.2-12. The critical value of t at the 0.10 level of significance with 60 degrees of freedom is 1.296. All explanatory variables with t values less than 1.296 are not significant at the 0.10 level. Drop these variables from the equation and rerun the corc-adjusted equations.

>*LOAD WF5-2-11*
>*SMPL 65.3 83.4*
>*LS NCN1 C RCUN(-1) RITO(-1) AR(1)*

```
SMPL  1965.3 - 1983.4
74 Observations
LS // Dependent Variable is NCN1
Convergence achieved after 1 iterations
============================================================
      VARIABLE   COEFFICIENT  STD. ERROR    T-STAT.   2-TAIL SIG.
============================================================
           C    140722.14    11726.875    11.999970   0.000
     RCUN(-1)   -117.36236   36.438560    -3.2208286  0.002
     RITO(-1)   350.03045    131.32401    2.6653957   0.010
- - - - - - - - - - - - - - - - - - - - - - - - - - - - - - - -
      AR(1)     0.3264320    0.1121663    2.9102511   0.005
============================================================
R-squared            0.316051   Mean of dependent var   114713.3
Adjusted R-squared   0.286738   S.D. of dependent var   12719.94
S.E. of regression   10742.60   Sum of squared resid    8.08D+09
Durbin-Watson stat   1.785759   F-statistic             10.78225
Log likelihood       -789.8113
============================================================
```

101

>*LS NMN1 C RCUN(-1) RITO(-1) AR(1)*

```
SMPL  1965.3 - 1983.4
74 Observations
LS // Dependent Variable is NMN1
Convergence achieved after 2 iterations
```

VARIABLE	COEFFICIENT	STD. ERROR	T-STAT.	2-TAIL SIG.
C	1392108.1	56334.282	24.711562	0.000
RCUN(-1)	-1115.4358	118.54045	-9.4097484	0.000
RITO(-1)	1865.1251	377.20165	4.9446367	0.000
AR(1)	0.7841921	0.0618333	12.682362	0.000

R-squared	0.968002	Mean of dependent var	865787.3
Adjusted R-squared	0.966631	S.D. of dependent var	91295.76
S.E. of regression	16677.20	Sum of squared resid	1.95D+10
Durbin-Watson stat	1.606712	F-statistic	705.8833
Log likelihood	-822.3584		

>*LS NWR1 C RCUN(-1) RITO(-1) RGDE(-1) AR(1)*

```
SMPL  1965.3 - 1983.4
74 Observations
LS // Dependent Variable is NWR1
Convergence achieved after 3 iterations
```

VARIABLE	COEFFICIENT	STD. ERROR	T-STAT.	2-TAIL SIG.
C	364775.96	25522.000	14.292609	0.000
RCUN(-1)	311.69796	47.874950	6.5106691	0.000
RITO(-1)	315.61465	179.27740	1.7604820	0.083
RGDE(-1)	359.53108	258.19265	1.3924915	0.169
AR(1)	0.2868105	0.1118197	2.5649365	0.013

R-squared	0.932178	Mean of dependent var	695948.3
Adjusted R-squared	0.928246	S.D. of dependent var	51770.59
S.E. of regression	13867.74	Sum of squared resid	1.33D+10
Durbin-Watson stat	2.245998	F-statistic	237.0919
Log likelihood	-808.1747		

>*LS NSR1 C RCUN(-1) RITO(-1) RGDE(-1) AR(1)*

```
SMPL   1965.3 - 1983.4
74 Observations
LS // Dependent Variable is NSR1
Convergence achieved after 3 iterations
====================================================================
     VARIABLE    COEFFICIENT   STD. ERROR    T-STAT.    2-TAIL SIG.
====================================================================
           C      -63272.510   29106.799    -2.1738052    0.033
      RCUN(-1)     807.21488    50.470574    15.993773     0.000
      RITO(-1)    -438.22319   190.65329    -2.2985346     0.025
      RGDE(-1)    1194.8399    283.13158     4.2200871     0.000
--------------------------------------------------------------------
        AR(1)     0.5594410     0.1099367    5.0887559     0.000
====================================================================
R-squared              0.987611   Mean of dependent var    577493.5
Adjusted R-squared     0.986892   S.D. of dependent var    87732.21
S.E. of regression     10044.33   Sum of squared resid     6.96D+09
Durbin-Watson stat     1.635113   F-statistic              1375.071
Log likelihood         -784.3055
====================================================================
```

5.2-13.   Similar to Exercise 5.2-8, generate CONTO1 and the OLSQ forecast for NTO1 (OLNTO1) and plot.

>*FETCH NTO1 GNP PDE*
>*GENR RGNP=GNP/PDE*
>*SMPL 65.2 83.4*
>*LS NTO1 C RGNP(-1)*

```
SMPL   1965.2 - 1983.4
75 Observations
LS // Dependent Variable is NTO1
====================================================================
     VARIABLE    COEFFICIENT   STD. ERROR    T-STAT.    2-TAIL SIG.
====================================================================
           C     2305782.7    47662.445    48.377349     0.000
      RGNP(-1)    583.40160    37.754326    15.452576     0.000
====================================================================
R-squared              0.765862   Mean of dependent var    3033848.
Adjusted R-squared     0.762655   S.D. of dependent var    127916.1
S.E. of regression     62318.31   Sum of squared resid     2.84D+11
Durbin-Watson stat     0.563561   F-statistic              238.7821
Log likelihood         -933.4076
====================================================================
```

103

>*EXPAND 65.1 83.4*
>*DATA RGNP*

OBS.	RGNP
1965.1	*N84.1*
1984.1	*1595*
1984.2	*1601*
1984.3	*1616*
1984.4	*END*

>*SMPL 84.1 84.4*
>*FORCST OLNTO1*
>*SMPL 65.3 83.4*
>*LS NTO1 C RGNP(-1) AR(1)*

```
SMPL  1965.3 - 1983.4
74 Observations
LS // Dependent Variable is NTO1
Convergence achieved after 1 iterations
=======================================================================
        VARIABLE   COEFFICIENT   STD. ERROR    T-STAT.   2-TAIL SIG.
=======================================================================
            C       2357473.6    103095.85   22.866815    0.000
      RGNP(-1)      548.04637    80.255232    6.8287931    0.000
- - - - - - - - - - - - - - - - - - - - - - - - - - - - - - - - - - - -
         AR(1)      0.6739675    0.0801162    8.4123748    0.000
=======================================================================
R-squared              0.880644   Mean of dependent var    3038611.
Adjusted R-squared     0.877282   S.D. of dependent var    121910.0
S.E. of regression     42706.40   Sum of squared resid     1.29D+11
Durbin-Watson stat     2.045784   F-statistic              261.9306
Log likelihood         -892.4659
=======================================================================
```

>*SMPL 84.1 84.4*
>*FORCST CONTO1*
>*PLOT(A) CONTO1 OLNTO1*

5.3 Exercises

Questions for Review:

5.3-1.   The parameter estimates are unbiased since there is no general tendency for heteroscedasticity to cause an estimated slope parameter to be higher or lower than its actual value. But the parameter estimates are inefficient in the sense that the variances are biased and no longer at a minimum level.

5.3-2.   Equation (5.2-3), which is used in deriving the formula for s_{b_1} in equation (5.2-7), reduces to

$$\sigma_{\hat{b}_1}^2 = \sigma_e^2 \frac{(x_t - \bar{x})^2}{\Sigma((x_t - \bar{x})^2)^2}$$

only if the variances of each of the error terms in equation (5.2-3) are equal to σ_e^2. This is not the case, however, when heteroscedasticity is present in an equation.

5.3-3   When time-series rather than cross-section data are used in regression analysis, the likelihood of heteroscedasticity is reduced since changes in the various time-series variables tend to be roughly the same.

5.3-4.   When average annual percentage changes are used to express variables in relative terms, the presence of heteroscedasticity might be removed. In addition, year-to-year percentage changes tend to remove the seasonal component that may be present in a series.

5.3-5.   By confronting rather than ignoring econometric problems, strategic approaches are made available that help limit and direct attention to the avenues that can be taken to more accurately specify behavioral relationships.

Computer Exercises:

5.3-6.
>*FETCH NCN1 INR IRE GDE PDE*
>*GENR ITO=INR+IRE*
>*GENR RGDE=GDE/PDE*
>*GENR RITO=ITO/PDE*
>*SMPL 65.3 83.4*
>*LS NCN1 C RITO(-1) RGDE(-1) AR(1)*
>*GENR NCN1RE=RESID*
>*GRAPH NCN1RE RITO(-1)*

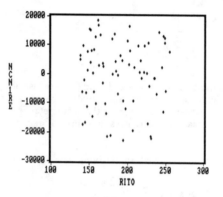

>*PLOT(A) NCN1RE*

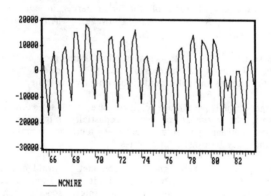

 NCN1RE

The scatter diagram suggests that the points are randomly distributed. The residuals do not show any systematic relationship with RITO(-1). Heteroscedasticity, therefore, does not appear to be present.

5.3-7.   Continue from the previous exercise.   After estimating the regression equation over the entire sample period, estimate an equation on the first one-third of the sample period and another on the last one-third of the sample period.

>*SMPL 65.3 83.4*
>*LS NCN1 C RITO(-1) RGDE(-1) AR(1)*

SMPL 1965.3 - 1983.4
74 Observations
LS // Dependent Variable is NCN1
Convergence achieved after 3 iterations
==
VARIABLE	COEFFICIENT	STD. ERROR	T-STAT.	2-TAIL SIG.
C	125594.08	27879.941	4.5048185	0.000
RITO(-1)	-38.293450	74.664534	-0.5128734	0.610
RGDE(-1)	-47.140228	262.97033	-0.1792606	0.858
AR(1)	0.4802811	0.1044355	4.5988305	0.000

R-squared	0.237829	Mean of dependent var	114713.3
Adjusted R-squared	0.205164	S.D. of dependent var	12719.94
S.E. of regression	11340.27	Sum of squared resid	9.00D+09
Durbin-Watson stat	1.786832	F-statistic	7.280967
Log likelihood	-793.8179		
==

107

>*SMPL 65.3 72.2*
>*LS NCN1 C RITO(-1) RGDE(-1) AR(1)*

```
SMPL   1965.3 - 1972.2
28 Observations
LS // Dependent Variable is NCN1
Convergence achieved after 1 iterations
```

==
VARIABLE	COEFFICIENT	STD. ERROR	T-STAT.	2-TAIL SIG.
==
C	8358.3972	41164.212	0.2030501	0.841
RITO(-1)	480.00672	213.71461	2.2460173	0.034
RGDE(-1)	456.97582	257.26423	1.7762898	0.088
- -
| AR(1) | 0.1152763 | 0.2043898 | 0.5640020 | 0.578 |
==

R-squared	0.286691	Mean of dependent var	119210.7
Adjusted R-squared	0.197527	S.D. of dependent var	11464.06
S.E. of regression	10269.60	Sum of squared resid	2.53D+09
Durbin-Watson stat	1.832612	F-statistic	3.215331
Log likelihood	-296.2066		
==

>*SMPL 77.1 83.4*
>*LS NCN1 C RITO(-1) RGDE(-1) AR(1)*

```
SMPL   1977.1 - 1983.4
28 Observations
LS // Dependent Variable is NCN1
Convergence achieved after 1 iterations
```

==
VARIABLE	COEFFICIENT	STD. ERROR	T-STAT.	2-TAIL SIG.
==
C	77873.849	53098.596	1.4665896	0.155
RITO(-1)	282.51906	177.13019	1.5949797	0.124
RGDE(-1)	-419.53628	300.01001	-1.3984076	0.175
- -
| AR(1) | 0.2018728 | 0.2000535 | 1.0090944 | 0.323 |
==

R-squared	0.339138	Mean of dependent var	110617.2
Adjusted R-squared	0.256530	S.D. of dependent var	12949.17
S.E. of regression	11165.38	Sum of squared resid	2.99D+09
Durbin-Watson stat	1.697558	F-statistic	4.105395
Log likelihood	-298.5482		
==

H_0: Homoscedasticity is present
H_1: Heteroscedasticity is present

Given: n = 74, m = 18, k = 2   df = (74 - 18 - 2(2))/2 = 26

At a 0.01 level of significance the critical value of F is 2.62, and at the 0.05 level of significance the critical value of F is 1.96.

$$F_m = 2,990/2,530 = 1.18$$

The residuals indicate the presence of homoscedasticity at both the 0.01 and 0.05 levels of significance.

5.3-8.   >*EDIT BA5-3-8*

```
1:   LOAD CS5-1-3
2:   SMPL 65.1 83.4
3:   GENR REXT=EXT/PDE
4:   GENR RIMP=IMP/PDE
5:   d ext imp pde ncn nnd nao nod nrt nsr nto
6.   fetch ncn1 nmn1 nwr1 nsr1
7:   SMPL 66.1 83.4
8:   GENR PRCUN=((RCUN-RCUN(-4))/ABS(RCUN(-4)))*100
9:   GENR PRITO=((RITO-RITO(-4))/ABS(RITO(-4)))*100
10:  GENR PRGDE=((RGDE-RGDE(-4))/ABS(RGDE(-4)))*100
11:  GENR PREXT=((REXT-REXT(-4))/ABS(REXT(-4)))*100
12:  GENR PRIMP=((RIMP-RIMP(-4))/ABS(RIMP(-4)))*100
13:  d rcun rito rgde rext rimp
14:  GENR PNCN1=((NCN1-NCN1(-4))/ABS(NCN1(-4)))*100
15:  GENR PNMN1=((NMN1-NMN1(-4))/ABS(NMN1(-4)))*100
16:  GENR PNWR1=((NWR1-NWR1(-4))/ABS(NWR1(-4)))*100
17:  GENR PNSR1=((NSR1-NSR1(-4))/ABS(NSR1(-4)))*100
18:  SMPL 66.3 83.4
19:  LS(P) PNCN1 C PRITO(-1) PRGDE(-1) AR(1)
20:  GENR PNCN1R=RESID
21:  LS(P) PNMN1 C PRCUN(-1) PREXT(-1) PRIMP(-1) PRITO(-1) PRGDE(-1) AR(1)
22:  GENR PNMN1R=RESID
23:  LS(P) PNWR1 C PRCUN(-1) PREXT(-1) PRIMP(-1) AR(1)
24:  GENR PNWR1R=RESID
25:  LS(P) PNSR1 C PRCUN(-1) PREXT(-1) PRIMP(-1) AR(1)
26:  GENR PNSR1R=RESID
27:  .XBA5-3-8
```

>*RUN BA5-3-8*

```
SMPL   1966.3 - 1983.4
70 Observations
LS // Dependent Variable is PNCN1
Convergence achieved after 3 iterations
=====================================================================
     VARIABLE    COEFFICIENT   STD. ERROR     T-STAT.    2-TAIL SIG.
=====================================================================
       C         -0.3594119    2.4509630    -0.1466411     0.884
    PRITO(-1)     0.2398079    0.1212533     1.9777434     0.052
    PRGDE(-1)     0.0035966    0.1767053     0.0203538     0.984
---------------------------------------------------------------------
    AR(1)         0.7994530    0.0746970    10.702615      0.000
=====================================================================
R-squared                0.712791   Mean of dependent var   -0.010267
Adjusted R-squared       0.699736   S.D. of dependent var    7.367378
S.E. of regression       4.037058   Sum of squared resid    1075.657
Durbin-Watson stat       1.705183   F-statistic             54.59914
Log likelihood        -194.9524
=====================================================================
```

```
SMPL   1966.3 - 1983.4
70 Observations
LS // Dependent Variable is PNMN1
Convergence achieved after 5 iterations
=====================================================================
     VARIABLE    COEFFICIENT   STD. ERROR     T-STAT.    2-TAIL SIG.
=====================================================================
       C         -4.6172766    1.5834763    -2.9159114     0.005
    PRCUN(-1)     0.8392161    0.2707075     3.1000842     0.003
    PREXT(-1)     0.0451201    0.0575046     0.7846347     0.436
    PRIMP(-1)    -0.0197491    0.0496623    -0.3976684     0.692
    PRITO(-1)     0.1367073    0.0796165     1.7170715     0.091
    PRGDE(-1)    -0.0917002    0.0963954    -0.9512921     0.345
---------------------------------------------------------------------
    AR(1)         0.8327078    0.0711054    11.710899      0.000
=====================================================================
R-squared                0.852985   Mean of dependent var   -1.592284
Adjusted R-squared       0.838983   S.D. of dependent var    4.941954
S.E. of regression       1.983053   Sum of squared resid     247.7474
Durbin-Watson stat       1.435383   F-statistic             60.92110
Log likelihood        -143.5627
=====================================================================
```

SMPL 1966.3 - 1983.4
70 Observations
LS // Dependent Variable is PNWR1
Convergence achieved after 2 iterations
===

VARIABLE	COEFFICIENT	STD. ERROR	T-STAT.	2-TAIL SIG.
C	0.3177853	0.8593031	0.3698175	0.713
PRCUN(-1)	0.2943270	0.1444094	2.0381429	0.046
PREXT(-1)	0.0237959	0.0357722	0.6652062	0.508
PRIMP(-1)	0.0310734	0.0312406	0.9946494	0.324
AR(1)	0.7983647	0.0870193	9.1745681	0.000

R-squared	0.714062	Mean of dependent var	1.471266
Adjusted R-squared	0.696466	S.D. of dependent var	2.310340
S.E. of regression	1.272856	Sum of squared resid	105.3106
Durbin-Watson stat	1.523537	F-statistic	40.58056
Log likelihood	-113.6204		

===

SMPL 1966.3 - 1983.4
70 Observations
LS // Dependent Variable is PNSR1
Convergence achieved after 1 iterations
===

VARIABLE	COEFFICIENT	STD. ERROR	T-STAT.	2-TAIL SIG.
C	2.6072518	0.7301616	3.5707874	0.001
PRCUN(-1)	0.1045799	0.1473897	0.7095465	0.481
PREXT(-1)	-0.0119098	0.0344706	-0.3455046	0.731
PRIMP(-1)	0.0444898	0.0296198	1.5020312	0.138
AR(1)	0.7503638	0.1013856	7.4010858	0.000

R-squared	0.537257	Mean of dependent var	3.033007
Adjusted R-squared	0.508781	S.D. of dependent var	1.792161
S.E. of regression	1.256073	Sum of squared resid	102.5517
Durbin-Watson stat	1.896178	F-statistic	18.86671
Log likelihood	-112.6912		

===

>*GRAPH PNCNIR PRITO(-1)*

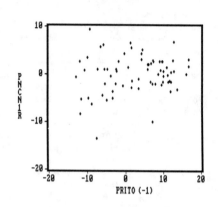

>*GRAPH PNMNIR PRITO(-1)*

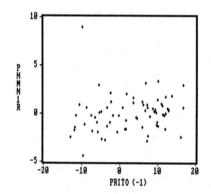

>*GRAPH PNWRIR PRIMP(-1)*

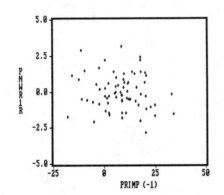

>*GRAPH PNSRIR PRIMP(-1)*

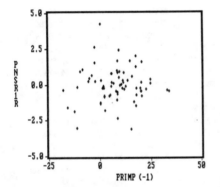

5.3-9.   Follow the procedures described in Computer Session 5.3-3 and print
PNSR, PRCUN, PREXT and PRIMP.   Rank and enter the data according
to the magnitude of PRCUN and run the necessary regressions.

>*SMPL 66.1 83.4*
>*PRINT PNRT PRCUN PREXT PRIMP*

obs	PNRT	PRCUN	PREXT	PRIMP
1966.1	9.994201	6.367621	14.60138	20.54134
1966.2	13.91386	4.945393	-0.472481	9.529882
1966.3	13.18721	5.009129	3.025268	15.62556
1966.4	12.47834	2.438662	4.351347	11.54595
1967.1	6.379613	1.525954	5.894334	9.117002
1967.2	4.274207	3.346697	4.196107	5.687201
1967.3	5.285714	2.200867	1.211773	0.069212
1967.4	9.090909	2.472645	1.459436	4.343630
1968.1	13.66265	4.262134	1.095451	8.539043
1968.2	10.94120	3.979071	5.819291	11.81740
1968.3	10.05578	5.718405	10.80274	17.62457
1968.4	9.039548	5.539006	6.114883	11.00771
1969.1	9.549418	4.397867	-4.687488	-4.077727
1969.2	13.07375	3.803605	8.661017	12.48738
1969.3	10.31507	1.799052	3.752552	5.500845
1969.4	8.031088	2.268536	9.656077	7.716671
1970.1	9.101765	1.543464	20.96368	17.59195
1970.2	5.190398	1.097883	6.881266	0.184452
1970.3	4.768409	2.041247	5.888199	2.172609
1970.4	4.040767	1.043984	1.876984	2.160033
1971.1	2.724067	2.272490	2.409056	1.726286
1971.2	3.381123	2.736022	-1.413910	6.529426
1971.3	5.926277	2.579039	3.300182	8.343172
1971.4	5.912182	4.335827	-4.765444	1.188449
1972.1	6.665088	3.944209	3.452851	16.47313
1972.2	9.060441	5.118133	2.805539	8.584062
1972.3	5.818507	5.758004	4.593099	8.473736
1972.4	6.093580	6.216029	22.21633	22.46425
1973.1	5.249723	6.756004	24.14026	14.60484
1973.2	6.389742	4.777374	35.03701	19.92221
1973.3	8.882309	3.765809	37.65869	17.60045
1973.4	4.994872	1.572172	37.12574	17.83234
1974.1	6.327112	0.397336	32.77636	20.10219
1974.2	4.910358	1.010018	28.61440	32.88261
1974.3	5.885209	1.105900	18.29066	33.81159
1974.4	9.280063	-0.541895	13.34076	24.50971
1975.1	5.028266	-1.223433	2.750357	2.358900
1975.2	3.076047	-0.192636	-6.999846	-18.22481
1975.3	3.393561	0.556780	-4.859255	-15.98767
1975.4	4.290695	3.311607	-2.494998	-12.55670
1976.1	9.348442	5.817501	-0.721214	5.524696
1976.2	10.00276	5.183269	6.971647	20.45185
1976.3	8.755433	5.137352	8.374403	20.38943
1976.4	7.825491	5.985583	4.762506	20.05100

114

1977.1	7.487047	5.547312	3.178737	17.58962
1977.2	8.666164	5.038968	3.820482	15.01912
1977.3	10.08972	4.760160	1.392973	9.290698
1977.4	11.76471	4.592776	-3.795080	8.143888
1978.1	12.61348	3.485142	3.645772	8.511618
1978.2	12.47265	4.684675	7.487385	8.558420
1978.3	10.66681	4.285999	11.24533	10.46251
1978.4	9.507113	3.933023	23.17025	10.87280
1979.1	7.369623	3.680167	19.80220	5.499499
1979.2	4.818213	2.037314	15.77857	9.738860
1979.3	4.039045	2.892171	19.43970	13.37920
1979.4	6.191587	3.381829	18.58321	19.56106
1980.1	3.853821	3.351524	20.76756	24.52020
1980.2	3.856209	1.066554	15.18071	11.22574
1980.3	4.504505	0.908377	6.427866	0.288429
1980.4	2.018349	0.202357	0.977013	-2.569206
1981.1	3.561740	0.765200	-0.779958	-5.801175
1981.2	2.811202	3.437538	0.454610	1.526133
1981.3	3.304803	2.540308	-0.374094	4.981757
1981.4	1.718825	0.570868	-1.177183	-2.367417
1982.1	1.091019	0.393869	-8.915090	-8.573597
1982.2	0.815954	0.378439	-7.781412	-11.12716
1982.3	-1.133119	0.827716	-10.86942	-5.248527
1982.4	-0.864635	3.005112	-16.93958	-11.35966
1983.1	-0.122225	2.158999	-12.84754	-9.859701
1983.2	1.275046	4.569187	-13.77410	-2.638685
1983.3	2.934296	4.358411	-5.246809	0.126079
1983.4	3.546968	4.484963	5.202597	12.71440

==

>*CREATE*

(U) Undated
(A) Annual
(Q) Quarterly
(M) Monthly
Frequency? *U*

>*DATA PRCUNR PNRTR PREXTR PRIMPR*

==

obs	PRCUNR	PNRTR	PREXTR	PRIMPR
1	-1.223433	5.028266	2.750357	2.358900
2	-0.541895	9.280063	13.34076	24.50971
3	-0.192636	3.076047	-6.999846	-18.22481
4	0.202357	2.018349	0.977013	-2.569206

115

5	0.378439	0.815954	-7.781412	-11.12716
6	0.393869	1.091019	-8.915090	-8.573597
7	0.397336	6.327112	32.77636	20.10219
8	0.556780	3.393561	-4.859255	-15.98767
9	0.570868	1.718825	-1.177183	-2.367417
10	0.765200	3.561740	-0.779958	-5.801175
11	0.827716	-1.133119	-10.86942	-5.248527
12	0.908377	4.504505	6.427866	0.288429
13	1.010018	4.910358	28.61440	32.88261
14	1.043984	4.040767	1.876984	2.160033
15	1.066554	3.856209	15.18071	11.22574
16	1.097883	5.190398	6.881266	0.184452
17	1.105900	5.885209	18.29066	33.81159
18	1.525954	6.379613	5.894334	9.117002
19	1.543464	9.101765	20.96368	17.59195
20	1.572172	4.994872	37.12574	17.83234
21	1.799052	10.31507	3.752552	5.500845
22	2.037314	4.818213	15.77857	9.738860
23	2.041247	4.768409	5.888199	2.172609
24	2.158999	-0.122225	-12.84754	-9.859701
25	2.200867	5.285714	1.211773	0.069212
26	2.268536	8.031088	9.656077	7.716671
27	2.272490	2.724067	2.409056	1.726286
28	2.438662	12.47834	4.351347	11.54595
29	2.472645	9.090909	1.459436	4.343630
30	2.540308	3.304803	-0.374094	4.981757
31	2.579039	5.926277	3.300182	8.343172
32	2.736022	3.381123	-1.413910	6.529426
33	2.892171	4.039045	19.43970	13.37920
34	3.005112	-0.864635	-16.93958	-11.35966
35	3.311607	4.290695	-2.494998	-12.55670
36	3.346697	4.274207	4.196107	5.687201
37	3.351524	3.853821	20.76756	24.52020
38	3.381829	6.191587	18.58321	19.56106
39	3.437538	2.811202	0.454610	1.526133
40	3.485142	12.61348	3.645772	8.511618
41	3.680167	7.369623	19.80220	5.499499
42	3.765809	8.882309	37.65869	17.60045
43	3.803605	13.07375	8.661017	12.48738
44	3.933023	9.507113	23.17025	10.87280
45	3.944209	6.665088	3.452851	16.47313
46	3.979071	10.94120	5.819291	11.81740
47	4.262134	13.66265	1.095451	8.539043
48	4.285999	10.66681	11.24533	10.46251
49	4.335827	5.912182	-4.765444	1.188449
50	4.358411	2.934296	-5.246809	0.126079
51	4.397867	9.549418	-4.687488	-4.077727

52	4.484963	3.546968	5.202597	12.71440
53	4.569187	1.275046	-13.77410	-2.638685
54	4.592776	11.76471	-3.795080	8.143888
55	4.684675	12.47265	7.487385	8.558420
56	4.760160	10.08972	1.392973	9.290698
57	4.777374	6.389742	35.03701	19.92221
58	4.945393	13.91386	-0.472481	9.529882
59	5.009129	13.18721	3.025268	15.62556
60	5.038968	8.666164	3.820482	15.01912
61	5.118133	9.060441	2.805539	8.584062
62	5.137352	8.755433	8.374403	20.38943
63	5.183269	10.00276	6.971647	20.45185
64	5.539006	9.039548	6.114883	11.00771
65	5.547312	7.487047	3.178737	17.58962
66	5.718405	10.05578	10.80274	17.62457
67	5.758004	5.818507	4.593099	8.473736
68	5.817501	9.348442	-0.721214	5.524696
69	5.985583	7.825491	4.762506	20.05100
70	6.216029	6.093580	22.21633	22.46425
71	6.367621	9.994201	14.60138	20.54134
72	6.756004	5.249723	24.14026	14.60484

==

>*SMPL 3 29*
>*LS PNRTR C PREXTR(-1) PRIMPR(-1) PRCUNR(-1) AR(1)*

SMPL   3 -   29
27 Observations
LS // Dependent Variable is PNRTR
Convergence achieved after 4 iterations
==

VARIABLE	COEFFICIENT	STD. ERROR	T-STAT.	2-TAIL SIG.
C	2.5818113	0.8262632	3.1246837	0.005
PREXTR(-1)	-0.0306240	0.0802273	-0.3817149	0.706
PRIMPR(-1)	0.1130449	0.0836768	1.3509714	0.190
PRCUNR(-1)	1.5769738	0.5956536	2.6474680	0.015
AR(1)	-0.2239702	0.2154358	-1.0396144	0.310

==

R-squared	0.324249	Mean of dependent var	4.708251
Adjusted R-squared	0.201385	S.D. of dependent var	3.171904
S.E. of regression	2.834580	Sum of squared resid	176.7666
Durbin-Watson stat	2.033697	F-statistic	2.639091
Log likelihood	-63.67775		

==

```
>SMPL 46 72
>LS PNRTR C PREXTR(-1) PRIMPR(-1) PRCUNR(-1) AR(1)

SMPL     46  -    72
27 Observations
LS // Dependent Variable is PNRTR
Convergence achieved after 3 iterations
====================================================================
       VARIABLE   COEFFICIENT  STD. ERROR    T-STAT.   2-TAIL SIG.
====================================================================
          C        14.194012   5.5385607    2.5627619    0.018
      PREXTR(-1)   0.0276174   0.1036053    0.2665631    0.792
      PRIMPR(-1)   0.0773780   0.1446833    0.5348095    0.598
      PRCUNR(-1)  -1.3146689   1.1822585   -1.1119979    0.278
--------------------------------------------------------------------
       AR(1)       0.0717057   0.2165098    0.3311894    0.744
====================================================================
R-squared              0.084708   Mean of dependent var   8.655688
Adjusted R-squared    -0.081709   S.D. of dependent var   3.223812
S.E. of regression     3.352934   Sum of squared resid    247.3276
Durbin-Watson stat     1.892093   F-statistic             0.509009
Log likelihood       -68.21218
====================================================================
```

From the output:

$$F_m = \frac{SSR_{46-72}}{SSR_{3-29}} = \frac{247.3}{176.8} = 1.40$$

The computed F value is the same as the figure reported in Table 5.3-2.

6.1 Exercises

Questions for Review:

6.1-1. From Exercise 5.3-8:

$$PNCN1 = -0.36 + 0.24 \; PRITO(-1) \quad + 0.003 \; PRGDE(-1)$$
$$\quad\quad (0.15) \; (1.98) \quad\quad\quad\quad\quad (0.02)$$

$R^2 = 0.71$	$\overline{R}^2 = 0.70$	$s_e = 4.04$	$F_m = 54.6$
$DW_m = 1.70$	$AR(1) = 0.80$	$n = 70$ from 1966:3 to 1983:4	

$$PNMN1 = -4.62 + 0.84 \; PRCUN(-1) + 0.04 \; PREXT(-1) - 0.02 \; PRIMP(-1)$$
$$\quad\quad (2.91) \; (3.10) \quad\quad\quad\quad (0.78) \quad\quad\quad\quad\quad (0.40)$$

$$+ 0.14 \; PRITO(-1) - 0.10 \; PRGDE(-1)$$
$$\quad (1.72) \quad\quad\quad\quad (0.95)$$

$R^2 = 0.85$	$\overline{R}^2 = 0.84$	$s_e = 1.98$	$F_m = 60.9$
$DW_m = 1.43$	$AR(1) = 0.83$	$n = 70$ from 1966:3 to 1983:4	

$$PNWR1 = 0.32 \quad + 0.30 \; PRCUN(-1) + 0.02 \; PREXT(-1) + 0.03 \; PRIMP(-1)$$
$$\quad\quad (0.37) \quad (2.04) \quad\quad\quad\quad (0.66) \quad\quad\quad\quad\quad (0.99)$$

$R^2 = 0.71$	$\overline{R}^2 = 0.70$	$s_e = 1.27$	$F_m = 40.58$
$DW_m = 1.52$	$AR(1) = 0.80$	$n = 70$ from 1966:3 to 1983:4	

$$PNSR1 = 2.61 \quad + 0.10 \; PRCUN(-1) - 0.01 \; PREXT(-1) + 0.04 \; PRIMP(-1)$$
$$\quad\quad (3.57) \quad (0.71) \quad\quad\quad\quad (0.34) \quad\quad\quad\quad\quad (1.50)$$

$R^2 = 0.54$	$\overline{R}^2 = 0.51$	$s_e = 1.26$	$F_m = 18.9$
$DW_m = 1.90$	$AR(1) = 0.75$	$n = 70$ from 1966:3 to 1983:4	

6.1-2. When the same variables in two regression relationships are expressed in different functional forms, the variables will change at different rates. Hence, the R^2 values which measure the association between the variables will be different even though the equations are measuring the associations between the same basic variables.

6.1-3. From Equation (6.1-3), $E_{NAO_t \cdot RGDE_{t-1}} = 0.34$.

From Equation (5.2-27), $E_{NAO_t \cdot RGDE_{t-1}} = 343.77(RGDE_{t-1}/NAO_t)$.

Thus, the elasticity based on the levels form of the equation will not be constant as in the percentage change form of the equation but will vary

119

with respect to the levels of $RGDE_{t-1}$ and NAO_t.

6.1-4. When the sample period is extended, the Phillips Curve takes on a looped pattern rather than a stable inverse functional relationship as depicted in Figure 6.1-11.

6.1-5. a. Output = f(Labor input)
        b. Interest = f(Time)
        c. Kilowatt hours used per hour = f(5:00 P.M. to 9:00 A.M.)
        d. Money demand = f(Interest rate)

Computer Exercises:

6.1-6. >*FETCH NAO ITO GDE PDE*
        >*GENR RITO=ITO/PDE*
        >*GENR RGDE=GDE/PDE*
        >*GENR LNAO=LOG(NAO)*
        >*GENR LRITO=LOG(RITO)*
        >*GENR LRGDE=LOG(RGDE)*
        >*SMPL 65.3 83.4*
        >*LS LNAO C LRITO(-1) LRGDE(-1) AR(1)*

```
SMPL  1965.3 - 1983.4
74 Observations
LS // Dependent Variable is LNAO
Convergence achieved after 5 iterations
====================================================================
      VARIABLE    COEFFICIENT   STD. ERROR    T-STAT.    2-TAIL SIG.
====================================================================
        C          7.6952368    0.8737498    8.8071397    0.000
     LRITO(-1)     0.3282233    0.1121448    2.9267806    0.005
     LRGDE(-1)     0.3919658    0.1393181    2.8134589    0.006
--------------------------------------------------------------------
      AR(1)        0.9331448    0.0486068    19.197829    0.000
====================================================================
R-squared            0.949806    Mean of dependent var   11.09627
Adjusted R-squared   0.947655    S.D. of dependent var    0.121192
S.E. of regression   0.027728    Sum of squared resid     0.053817
Durbin-Watson stat   1.381994    F-statistic            441.5301
Log likelihood     162.3688
====================================================================
```

The estimated regression equation is

$$LNAO = 7.695 + 0.328 \ LRITO(-1) + 0.392 \ LRGDE(-1)$$

From this equation

$$E_{NAO_t \cdot RGDE_{t-1}} = 0.39$$

where from equation (6.1-3) the elasticity is 0.34. The logarithmic specification generates a higher elasticity measurement since the changes are measured in continuous form rather than discrete form as is done when percentage changes are used to represent the variables.

6.1-7. >*DATA TIM*

[*Enter the values of TIM*]

>*FETCH NTO1*
>*GENR LNTO1=LOG(NTO1)*
>*LS NTO1 C TIM*

```
SMPL  1965.1 - 1983.4
76 Observations
LS // Dependent Variable is LNTO1
=======================================================================
      VARIABLE   COEFFICIENT  STD. ERROR   T-STAT.   2-TAIL SIG.
=======================================================================
         C       14.856801    0.0060931   2438.2863    0.000
         TIM      0.0017048    0.0001375    12.398076   0.000
=======================================================================
R-squared              0.675029   Mean of dependent var   14.92244
Adjusted R-squared     0.670637   S.D. of dependent var   0.045823
S.E. of regression     0.026298   Sum of squared resid    0.051176
Durbin-Watson stat     0.396518   F-statistic             153.7123
Log likelihood       169.6830
=======================================================================
```

>*FORCST FLNTO1*
>*PLOT(A) LNTO1 FLNTO1*

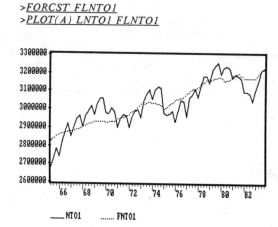

———NTO1   ······· FNTO1

>*GENR FNTO1=2.718^FLNTO1*
>*PLOT(A) NTO1 FNTO1*

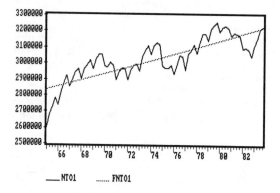

———NTO1   ······· FNTO1

>*SMPL 65.2 83.4*
>*LS LNTO1 C TIM AR(1)*

SMPL 1965.2 - 1983.4
75 Observations
LS // Dependent Variable is LNTO1
Convergence achieved after 2 iterations
==
VARIABLE	COEFFICIENT	STD. ERROR	T-STAT.	2-TAIL SIG.
==
| C | 14.875418 | 0.0144565 | 1028.9806 | 0.000 |
| TIM | 0.0013612 | 0.0003024 | 4.5014522 | 0.000 |

| AR(1) | 0.7271312 | 0.0660420 | 11.010140 | 0.000 |
==
R-squared	0.880323	Mean of dependent var	14.92445
Adjusted R-squared	0.876998	S.D. of dependent var	0.042598
S.E. of regression	0.014940	Sum of squared resid	0.016071
Durbin-Watson stat	2.036935	F-statistic	264.8086
Log likelihood	210.3890		
==

>*SMPL 65.1 83.4*
>*GENR STIM=TIM^2*
>*GENR CTIM=TIM^3*
>*LS NTO1 C TIM STIM CTIM*

SMPL 1965.1 - 1983.4
76 Observations
LS // Dependent Variable is NTO1
==
VARIABLE	COEFFICIENT	STD. ERROR	T-STAT.	2-TAIL SIG.
==
C	2724924.7	34785.227	78.335689	0.000
TIM	16925.284	3886.8169	4.3545359	0.000
STIM	-295.48316	116.88205	-2.5280456	0.014
CTIM	2.0574735	0.9981906	2.0612030	0.043
==
R-squared	0.731923	Mean of dependent var	3028143.
Adjusted R-squared	0.720754	S.D. of dependent var	136446.3
S.E. of regression	72103.34	Sum of squared resid	3.74D+11
Durbin-Watson stat	0.472232	F-statistic	65.52668
Log likelihood	-955.9098		
==

>*FORCST FNTO1*
>*PLOT(A) NTO1 FNTO1*

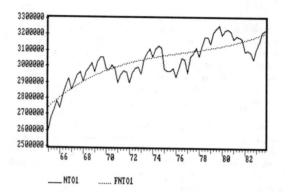

>*SMPL 65.2 83.4*
>*LS NTO1 C TIM STIM CTIM AR(1)*

SMPL 1965.2 - 1983.4
75 Observations
LS // Dependent Variable is NTO1
Convergence achieved after 3 iterations
==
VARIABLE	COEFFICIENT	STD. ERROR	T-STAT.	2-TAIL SIG.
C	2901785.3	141888.08	20.451226	0.000
TIM	2492.8404	12845.475	0.1940637	0.847
STIM	38.310353	335.29320	0.1142593	0.909
CTIM	-0.2543060	2.6017905	-0.0977427	0.922

....

| AR(1) | 0.7371716 | 0.0748223 | 9.8522972 | 0.000 |
==
R-squared	0.879007	Mean of dependent var	3033848.
Adjusted R-squared	0.872093	S.D. of dependent var	127916.1
S.E. of regression	45747.98	Sum of squared resid	1.47D+11
Durbin-Watson stat	2.030040	F-statistic	127.1367
Log likelihood	-908.6509		
==

>*FETCH GNP PDE*
>*SMPL 65.1 83.4*
>*GENR RGNP=GNP/PDE*
>*LS NTO1 C RGNP*

SMPL 1965.1 - 1983.4
76 Observations
LS // Dependent Variable is NTO1

==

VARIABLE	COEFFICIENT	STD. ERROR	T-STAT.	2-TAIL SIG.

==

| C | 2268395.0 | 52202.229 | 43.453988 | 0.000 |
| RGNP | 606.71717 | 41.201458 | 14.725624 | 0.000 |

==

R-squared	0.745568	Mean of dependent var	3028143.
Adjusted R-squared	0.742130	S.D. of dependent var	136446.3
S.E. of regression	69288.67	Sum of squared resid	3.55D+11
Durbin-Watson stat	0.498309	F-statistic	216.8440
Log likelihood	-953.9247		

==

>*FORCST FNTO1*
>*PLOT(A) NTO1 FNTO1*

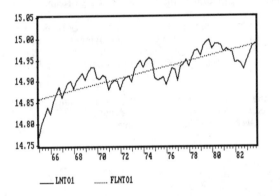

_____ LNTO1   .... FLNTO1

125

```
>SMPL 65.2 83.4
>LS NTO1 C RGNP AR(1)

SMPL  1965.2 - 1983.4
75 Observations
LS // Dependent Variable is NTO1
Convergence achieved after 2 iterations
========================================================================
      VARIABLE   COEFFICIENT   STD. ERROR   T-STAT.    2-TAIL SIG.
========================================================================
         C       2390081.8    108362.40    22.056377   0.000
        RGNP     518.68118    83.670241    6.1991119   0.000
------------------------------------------------------------------------
       AR(1)     0.6837761    0.0725704    9.4222440   0.000
========================================================================
R-squared            0.885432   Mean of dependent var   3033848.
Adjusted R-squared   0.882250   S.D. of dependent var   127916.1
S.E. of regression   43894.07   Sum of squared resid    1.39D+11
Durbin-Watson stat   2.102487   F-statistic             278.2250
Log likelihood       -906.6047
========================================================================
```

Similar to the Orange County results, the ordinary least square and the CORC-adjusted regression equations relating the lag of Chicago employment to time are significant at the 0.01 level of significance.

Also, the results emanating from the cubic polynmomial least squares regression equation relating Chicago employment to time is significant. This is similar to the Orange County results. Unlike the Orange County results, the cubic polynomial CORC-adjustment regression equation is not significant.

Similar to the Orange County results, when time is replaced by real GNP, the OSLQ and CORC-adjusted equations relating Chicago employment and real GNP show significant t values.

6.1-8.
```
>LOAD WF4-4-7
>SMPL 65.1 83.4
>GENR LRMNS=LOG(RMNS)
>GENR LNCN=LOG(NCN)
>GENR LBTO1=LOG(BTO1)
>GENR LBTO=LOG(BTO)
>GENR LNCN1=LOG(NCN1)
>GENR LPRR=LOG(PRR)
>SMPL 65.3 83.4
>LS LNCN C LBTO(-1) AR(1)
```

```
SMPL   1965.3 - 1983.4
74 Observations
LS // Dependent Variable is LNCN
Convergence achieved after 4 iterations
=====================================================================
     VARIABLE    COEFFICIENT   STD. ERROR    T-STAT.    2-TAIL SIG.
=====================================================================
        C         9.0382277    0.4367535    20.694118    0.000
     LBTO(-1)     0.1097765    0.0263809     4.1612142    0.000
---------------------------------------------------------------------
      AR(1)       0.9634803    0.0298906    32.233558     0.000
=====================================================================
R-squared              0.954175   Mean of dependent var   10.26865
Adjusted R-squared     0.952884   S.D. of dependent var    0.303517
S.E. of regression     0.065882   Sum of squared resid     0.308169
Durbin-Watson stat     1.851434   F-statistic            739.1901
Log likelihood        97.80190
=====================================================================
```

> *LS LNCN1 C LBTO1(-1) AR(1)*

```
SMPL   1965.3 - 1983.4
74 Observations
LS // Dependent Variable is LNCN1
Convergence achieved after 2 iterations
=====================================================================
     VARIABLE    COEFFICIENT   STD. ERROR    T-STAT.    2-TAIL SIG.
=====================================================================
        C        11.700055     0.3463739    33.778681    0.000
     LBTO1(-1)   -0.0046632    0.0287443    -0.1622316    0.872
---------------------------------------------------------------------
      AR(1)       0.4664749    0.1066686     4.3731220    0.000
=====================================================================
R-squared              0.217534   Mean of dependent var   11.64394
Adjusted R-squared     0.195492   S.D. of dependent var    0.113483
S.E. of regression     0.101788   Sum of squared resid     0.735610
Durbin-Watson stat     1.814512   F-statistic              9.869368
Log likelihood        65.61000
=====================================================================
```

>*LS LPRR C LRMNS(-1) AR(1)*

```
SMPL  1965.3 - 1983.4
74 Observations
LS // Dependent Variable is LPRR
Convergence achieved after 3 iterations
=====================================================================
       VARIABLE   COEFFICIENT  STD. ERROR    T-STAT.   2-TAIL SIG.
=====================================================================
          C       -19.696037    6.7633241   -2.9121830    0.005
      LRMNS(-1)     4.0518240    1.2443236    3.2562463    0.002
.....................................................................
       AR(1)        0.9664796    0.0290087   33.316882     0.000
=====================================================================
R-squared              0.933556   Mean of dependent var    2.128105
Adjusted R-squared     0.931684   S.D. of dependent var    0.393235
S.E. of regression     0.102781   Sum of squared resid     0.750042
Durbin-Watson stat     1.110037   F-statistic              498.7810
Log likelihood        64.89114
=====================================================================
```

>*SMPL 66.2 83.4*
>*LS LPRR C LRMNS(-4) AR(1)*

```
SMPL  1966.2 - 1983.4
71 Observations
LS // Dependent Variable is LPRR
Convergence achieved after 3 iterations
=====================================================================
       VARIABLE   COEFFICIENT  STD. ERROR    T-STAT.   2-TAIL SIG.
=====================================================================
          C        -9.8211095    7.5841955   -1.2949441    0.200
      LRMNS(-4)     2.2413153    1.3982947    1.6028919    0.114
.....................................................................
       AR(1)        0.9567708    0.0346038   27.649272     0.000
=====================================================================
R-squared              0.918858   Mean of dependent var    2.152231
Adjusted R-squared     0.916471   S.D. of dependent var    0.382844
S.E. of regression     0.110647   Sum of squared resid     0.832509
Durbin-Watson stat     1.575311   F-statistic              385.0160
Log likelihood        57.08803
=====================================================================
```

a.

$H_0: b_1 \leq 0$
$H_1: b_1 > 0$

$t_m = 4.16$ $t_c = 1.67$ $n = 75$ $df = 73$

128

Since t_m is greater than t_c, the null hypothesis is rejected and the alternative is accepted.

b.
$$H_0: b_1 \leq 0$$
$$H_1: b_1 > 0$$

$t_m = -0.162$ $t_c = 1.67$ $n = 75$ $df = 73$

Since t_m is less than t_c, the null hypothesis cannot be rejected at the 0.05 level of significance.

c.
$$H_0: b_1 \geq 0$$
$$H_1: b_1 < 0$$

$t_m = 3.26$ $t_c = 1.67$ $n = 75$ $df = 73$

Since $\hat{b}_1 > 0$, the null hypothesis cannot be rejected.

d.
$$H_0: b_1 = 0$$
$$H_1: b_1 \neq 0$$

$t_m = 1.60$ $t_c = 1.67$ $n = 75$ $df = 73$

Since t_m is less than t_c, the null hypothesis cannot be rejected.

Study Project:

6.1-9.   Test the semilogarithmic relationship between the prime interest rate and time.

>*FETCH PRR*
>*DATA TIM*

OBS.	TIM
1965.1	*1*
1965.2	*2*
1965.3	*3*
•	•
•	•
•	•
1983.2	*74*
1983.3	*75*
1983.4	*76*
1983.4	*END*

129

>*GENR LPRR=LOG(PRR)*
>*LS PRR C TIM*

```
SMPL  1965.1 - 1983.4
76 Observations
LS // Dependent Variable is PRR
======================================================================
     VARIABLE   COEFFICIENT  STD. ERROR    T-STAT.   2-TAIL SIG.
======================================================================
        C        3.7301400    0.6063931    6.1513561    0.000
       TIM       0.1365271    0.0136848    9.9765440    0.000
======================================================================
R-squared            0.573564   Mean of dependent var    8.986434
Adjusted R-squared   0.567802   S.D. of dependent var    3.980975
S.E. of regression   2.617164   Sum of squared resid     506.8666
Durbin-Watson stat   0.240264   F-statistic              99.53143
Log likelihood      -179.9449
======================================================================
```

>*LS LPRR C TIM*

```
SMPL  1965.1 - 1983.4
76 Observations
LS // Dependent Variable is LPRR
======================================================================
     VARIABLE   COEFFICIENT  STD. ERROR    T-STAT.   2-TAIL SIG.
======================================================================
        C        1.5514687    0.0558684   27.770034    0.000
       TIM       0.0145510    0.0012608   11.540968    0.000
======================================================================
R-squared            0.642847   Mean of dependent var    2.111683
Adjusted R-squared   0.638020   S.D. of dependent var    0.400776
S.E. of regression   0.241126   Sum of squared resid     4.302475
Durbin-Watson stat   0.209723   F-statistic              133.1939
Log likelihood       1.279301
======================================================================
```

At the 0.01 level of significance, t_c = 2.39. Since t_m for both linear and similogarithmic forms of the relationship are greater than t_c, it is appropriate to conclude that both are significant. The semilogarithmic specification, however, produces a higher R^2 and t_m.

6.2 Exercises

Questions for Review:

6.2-1.   For example, $PNAO_t$ = $f(PRGDE_{t-1}$ ... $PRGDE_{t-n})$ and $PNOD_t$ =

$f(PRITO_{t-1} \ldots PRITO_{t-n})$.

6.2-2.   Since changes are calculated over the same quarters of different years in equations where the variables are expressed in year-to-year percentage form, seasonal variation should generally be absent in such equations.

6.2-3.   Data on LRBTO, Q1DUM, Q2DUM and Q3DUM would have to be entered for 1984:1 before using the *FORCST* command to generate $LRBTO_{84:1}$.

6.2-4.   The large increase in federal workers needed to conduct the decennial census explains the increases.   This qualitative factor can be measured by adding a dummy variable to the equation where

$$CENDUM_t = 1 \text{ in } 1970:2 \text{ and } 1980:2, \text{ and}$$

$$CENDUM_t = 0 \text{ otherwise.}$$

6.2-5.   For example, dummy variables can be used to measure the impact of crime prevention programs on crime rates.   They can also be used to measure the impact of liquor control laws on crime rates.

6.2-6.   Although the equality holds in the first three quarters, it is violated in the fourth quarter:

$$Q1DUM_{80:4} \neq 1 - Q2DUM_{80:4} - Q3DUM_{80:4}$$

Computer Exercises:

6.2-7.   *>FETCH NCN BTO GDE PDE*
          >GENR RBTO=BTO/PDE
          >GENR RGDE=GDE/PDE
          >GENR LNCN=LOG(NCN)
          >GENR LRBTO=LOG(RBTO)
          >GENR LRGDE=LOG(RGDE)
          >DATA STDUM

          [Enter the new values]

          >LS LNCN C LRBTO LRBTO(-1) LRBTO(-2) LRBTO(-3) LRBTO(-4)
          LRBTO(-5) LRBTO(-6) LRBTO(-7) LORBTO(-8) LRBTO(-9)
          LRBTO(-10) STDUM AR(1)

```
SMPL  1967.4 - 1983.4
65 Observations
LS // Dependent Variable is LNCN
Convergence achieved after 5 iterations
```

VARIABLE	COEFFICIENT	STD. ERROR	T-STAT.	2-TAIL SIG.
C	-0.9768768	2.1062358	-0.4638022	0.645
LRBTO	0.1267088	0.0259327	4.8860561	0.000
LRBTO(-1)	0.1765128	0.0294489	5.9938689	0.000
LRBTO(-2)	0.1115345	0.0311798	3.5771443	0.001
LRBTO(-3)	0.0474935	0.0312941	1.5176513	0.135
LRBTO(-4)	0.0833380	0.0298504	2.7918511	0.007
LRBTO(-5)	0.0785701	0.0285260	2.7543290	0.008
LRBTO(-6)	0.0649892	0.0280436	2.3174347	0.025
LRBTO(-7)	0.0388157	0.0291353	1.3322588	0.189
LRBTO(-8)	0.0796665	0.0298856	2.6657135	0.010
LRBTO(-9)	0.0808301	0.0282185	2.8644410	0.006
LRBTO(-10)	0.0501877	0.0261482	1.9193547	0.061
STDUM	0.0646082	0.0402002	1.6071625	0.114
AR(1)	0.9691188	0.0413973	23.410214	0.000

R-squared	0.971653	Mean of dependent var	10.32729	
Adjusted R-squared	0.964427	S.D. of dependent var	0.272921	
S.E. of regression	0.051475	Sum of squared resid	0.135135	
Durbin-Watson stat	2.000528	F-statistic	134.4694	
Log likelihood	108.4848			

6.2-8.

```
>FETCH NCN1 BTO1 GDE PDE
>GENR RBTO1=BTO1/PDE
>GENR RGDE=GDE/PDE
>GENR LNCN1=LOG(NCN1)
>GENR LRBTO1=LOG(RBTO1)
>GENR LRGDE=LOG(RGDE)
>SMPL 68.2 83.4
>LS LNCN1 C LRBTO1 LRBTO1(-1) LRBTO1(-2) LRBTO1(-3)
 LRBTO1(-4) LRBTO1(-5) LRBTO1(-6) LRBTO1(-7) LRBTO1(-8)
 LRBTO1(-9) LRBTO1(-10) LRBTO1(-11) LRBTO1(-12)
 LRGDE(-1) AR(1)
```

```
SMPL  1968.2 - 1983.4
63 Observations
LS // Dependent Variable is LNCN1
Convergence achieved after 2 iterations
===================================================================
     VARIABLE   COEFFICIENT  STD. ERROR   T-STAT.   2-TAIL SIG.
===================================================================
         C       1.6238463   1.4459950   1.1229958    0.267
      LRBTO1     0.2893100   0.0344397   8.4004744    0.000
    LRBTO1(-1)   0.0702970   0.0331680   2.1194202    0.039
    LRBTO1(-2)  -0.0335566   0.0299186  -1.1215983    0.268
    LRBTO1(-3)   0.0243717   0.0201396   1.2101369    0.232
    LRBTO1(-4)   0.0401201   0.0221884   1.8081580    0.077
    LRBTO1(-5)   0.0478730   0.0216006   2.2162795    0.032
    LRBTO1(-6)   0.0417653   0.0215506   1.9380171    0.059
    LRBTO1(-7)   0.0093737   0.0198485   0.4722651    0.639
    LRBTO1(-8)   0.0398856   0.0200336   1.9909404    0.052
    LRBTO1(-9)   0.0670313   0.0212132   3.1598817    0.003
   LRBTO1(-10)   0.0248801   0.0213879   1.1632765    0.251
   LRBTO1(-11)  -0.0038905   0.0203634  -0.1910543    0.849
   LRBTO1(-12)   0.0416123   0.0195254   2.1311896    0.038
    LRGDE(-1)    0.5126703   0.1140946   4.4933810    0.000
-------------------------------------------------------------------
      AR(1)      0.3758949   0.1355107   2.7739143    0.008
===================================================================
R-squared              0.842276   Mean of dependent var   11.64878
Adjusted R-squared     0.791938   S.D. of dependent var   0.117984
S.E. of regression     0.053817   Sum of squared resid    0.136124
Durbin-Watson stat     1.700923   F-statistic             16.73255
Log likelihood         103.9326
===================================================================
```

Unlike the Orange County results, the coefficients for LRBTO(-12) and LRGDE(-1) are significant.

6.2-9.
>*FETCH NCN BTO PDE*
>*GENR RBTO=BTO/PDE*
>*SMPL 66.1 83.4*
>*GENR PNCN=((NCN-NCN(-4))/ABS(NCN(-4)))*100*
>*GENR PRBTO=((RBTO-RBTO(-4))/ABS(RBTO(-4)))*100*
>*SMPL 68.4 83.4*
>*LS PNCN C PRBTO PRBTO(-1) PRBTO(-2) PRBTO(-3) PRBTO(-4)*
>*PRBTO(-5) PRBTO(-6) PRBTO(-7) PRBTO(-8) PRBTO(-9)*
>*PRBTO(-10) AR(1)*

```
SMPL   1968.4 - 1983.4
61 Observations
LS // Dependent Variable is PNCN
Convergence achieved after 2 iterations
===================================================================
        VARIABLE    COEFFICIENT    STD. ERROR      T-STAT.   2-TAIL SIG.
===================================================================
           C        -0.7166134     3.6345303     -0.1971681    0.845
        PRBTO        0.0742690      0.0246465      3.0133677    0.004
      PRBTO(-1)      0.1546574      0.0252534      6.1242162    0.000
      PRBTO(-2)      0.0872017      0.0256259      3.4028769    0.001
      PRBTO(-3)      0.0580375      0.0236813      2.4507750    0.018
      PRBTO(-4)      0.0464605      0.0252034      1.8434228    0.071
      PRBTO(-5)      0.0787179      0.0250785      3.1388574    0.003
      PRBTO(-6)      0.0591266      0.0251563      2.3503702    0.023
      PRBTO(-7)      0.0579279      0.0231021      2.5074697    0.016
      PRBTO(-8)      0.0429663      0.0249051      1.7252002    0.091
      PRBTO(-9)      0.0458540      0.0245083      1.8709590    0.067
     PRBTO(-10)      0.0213034      0.0244927      0.8697834    0.389
- - - - - - - - - - - - - - - - - - - - - - - - - - - - - - - - - - -
        AR(1)        0.7939317      0.0875081      9.0726671    0.000
===================================================================
R-squared               0.896670    Mean of dependent var    4.762596
Adjusted R-squared      0.870838    S.D. of dependent var   15.70603
S.E. of regression      5.644617    Sum of squared resid  1529.361
Durbin-Watson stat      1.575245    F-statistic             34.71098
Log likelihood       -184.8181
===================================================================
```

6.2-10.   >*FETCH NRT CUN EXT IMP PDE*
            >*GENR LNRT=LOG(NRT)*
            >*GENR RCUN=CUN/PDE*
            >*GENR REXT=EXT/PDE*
            >*GENR RIMP=IMP/PDE*
            >*GENR LRCUN=LOG(RCUN)*
            >*GENR LREXT=LOG(REXT)*
            >*GENR LRIMP=LOG(RIMP)*
            >*DATA Q1DUM Q2DUM Q3DUM*

OBS.	Q1DUM	Q2DUM	Q3DUM
1965.1	*1*	*0*	*0*
1965.2	*0*	*1*	*0*
1965.3	*0*	*0*	*1*
1965.4	*0*	*0*	*0*
•	•	•	•
•	•	•	•
•	•	•	•
1983.3	*0*	*0*	*1*
1983.4	*0*	*0*	*0*
1983.4	*END*		

>*SMPL 65.3 83.4*
>*LS LNRT C LRCUN(-1) LREXT(-1) LRIMP(-1) Q1DUM Q2DUM*
Q3DUM AR(1)

SMPL 1965.3 - 1983.4
74 Observations
LS // Dependent Variable is LNRT
Convergence achieved after 12 iterations
===

VARIABLE	COEFFICIENT	STD. ERROR	T-STAT.	2-TAIL SIG.
C	9.5322980	1.6362948	5.8255383	0.000
LRCUN(-1)	0.4176190	0.2204139	1.8947035	0.063
LREXT(-1)	-0.0349592	0.0592987	-0.5895440	0.558
LRIMP(-1)	0.0345690	0.0544436	0.6349507	0.528
Q1DUM	-0.0415030	0.0030871	-13.444181	0.000
Q2DUM	-0.0245144	0.0034652	-7.0743782	0.000
Q3DUM	-0.0140644	0.0030048	-4.6806259	0.000
AR(1)	0.9827681	0.0063438	154.91679	0.000

===

R-squared	0.998380	Mean of dependent var	11.58660
Adjusted R-squared	0.998208	S.D. of dependent var	0.346855
S.E. of regression	0.014681	Sum of squared resid	0.014226
Durbin-Watson stat	1.997337	F-statistic	5811.557
Log likelihood	211.5996		

===

6.2-11.
>*FETCH GNP MNS GEX TFG*
>*GENR BUD=TFG-GEX*
>*SMPL 65.2 83.4*
>*GENR CGNP=((((GNP-GNP(-1))/ABS(GNP(-1)))+1)^4-1)*100*
>*GENR CMNS=((((MNS-MNS(-1))/ABS(MNS(-1)))+1)^4-1)*100*
>*GENR CBUD=((((BUD-BUD(-1))/ABS(BUD(-1)))+1)^4-1)*100*

135

>*SMPL 66.1 83.4*
>*LS CGNP C PDL(CMNS) PDL(CBUD)*

```
PDL Parameters for CMNS
Number of Lags? 3
Order of Polynomial? 2
Zero Constraints? 0

PDL Parameters for CBUD
Number of Lags? 3
Order of Polynomial? 2
Zero Constraints? 0

SMPL   1966.1 - 1983.4
72 Observations
LS // Dependent Variable is CGNP
```

VARIABLE	COEFFICIENT	STD. ERROR	T-STAT.	2-TAIL SIG.
C	3.6220093	1.7111036	2.1167680	0.038
PDL1	0.2345177	0.1464006	1.6018904	0.114
PDL2	0.3623357	0.2476518	1.4630851	0.148
PDL3	-0.1611888	0.0795539	-2.0261595	0.047
PDL4	-8.242D-09	1.968D-08	-0.4187886	0.677
PDL5	9.311D-09	3.159D-08	0.2947628	0.769
PDL6	-3.134D-09	1.007D-08	-0.3111229	0.757

R-squared	0.250093	Mean of dependent var	9.190913
Adjusted R-squared	0.180871	S.D. of dependent var	4.596808
S.E. of regression	4.160375	Sum of squared resid	1125.067
Durbin-Watson stat	1.785093	F-statistic	3.612907
Log likelihood	-201.1251		

Lag Distribution of CMNS			Lag	Coef	S.E.	T-Stat
|	:	*	|	0	0.23452	0.14640	1.60189
|	:	*|	1	0.43566	0.10573	4.12049
|	:	*	|	2	0.31443	0.10427	3.01563
|*	:	|	3	-0.12917	0.14602	-0.88464

```
          0                    Sum  0.85544  0.24983  3.42409
```

```
Lag Distribution of CBUD      Lag   Coef     S.E.    T-Stat
===========================================================================
| *                        :|  0  -8.2D-09  2.0D-08 -0.41879
|                      *    :|  1  -2.1D-09  1.5D-08 -0.13416
|                      *    :|  2  -2.2D-09  1.6D-08 -0.13799
|*                         :|  3  -8.5D-09  2.0D-08 -0.42200
---------------------------------------------------------------------------
                           0  Sum -2.1D-08  4.2D-08 -0.49529
===========================================================================
```

Study Project:

6.2-12.   >*FETCH NRT CUN EXT IMP PDE*
          >*SEAS(M) NRT SNRT*

Generate Factor Series? (Y/N?) $\underline{N}$

>*GENR LSNRT=LOG(SNRT)*
>*GENR RCUN=CUN/PDE*
>*GENR REXT=EXT/PDE*
>*GENR RIMP=IMP/PDE*
>*GENR LRCUN=LOG(RCUN)*
>*GENR LREXT=LOG(REXT)*
>*GENR LRIMP=LOG(RIMP)*
>*DATA Q1DUM Q2DUM Q3DUM*

[See Exercise 6.2-10]

>*SMPL 65.3 83.4*
>*LS LSNRT C LRCUN(-1) LREXT(-1) LRIMP(-1)*
  Q1DUM Q2DUM Q3DUM AR(1)

```
SMPL   1965.3 - 1983.4
74 Observations
LS // Dependent Variable is LSNRT
Convergence achieved after 12 iterations
=====================================================================
     VARIABLE    COEFFICIENT   STD. ERROR      T-STAT.    2-TAIL SIG.
=====================================================================
        C         9.5110101    1.6362738     5.8126030     0.000
    LRCUN(-1)     0.4176535    0.2204108     1.8948869     0.063
    LREXT(-1)    -0.0349422    0.0592979    -0.5892664     0.558
    LRIMP(-1)     0.0345484    0.0544429     0.6345812     0.528
     Q1DUM        0.0012462    0.0030870     0.4036933     0.688
     Q2DUM        0.0010359    0.0034652     0.2989447     0.766
     Q3DUM        0.0019488    0.0030048     0.6485637     0.519
- - - - - - - - - - - - - - - - - - - - - - - - - - - - - - - - - - -
     AR(1)        0.9827683    0.0063438   154.91709       0.000
=====================================================================
R-squared             0.998376   Mean of dependent var   11.58625
Adjusted R-squared    0.998204   S.D. of dependent var    0.346433
S.E. of regression    0.014681   Sum of squared resid     0.014225
Durbin-Watson stat    1.997259   F-statistic           5797.583
Log likelihood      211.6006
=====================================================================
```

As might be expected, the dummy variables representing seasonal change lose their significance after the retail trade employment series is seasonally adjusted.

6.3 Exercises

Questions for Review:

6.3-1.
$$D_t = a_0 + a_1Y_t + a_2P_{t-1} + a_3I_t$$

$$S_t = b_0 + b_1P_{t-1} + b_2R_t + b_3C_t$$

$$D_t = S_t$$

Although the recursive nature of the above system of equations removes the presumption of simultaneous-equation bias, the one period lag placed on the price variable may introduce specification error.

6.3-2. This error term assumption made it possible to drop the mean, $\mu_{e_t x_t}$, from equation (4.2-15) in constructing equations for $\hat{b}_0$ and $\hat{b}_1$ in the bivariate formulation presented in Section 4.2. Similarly, this assumption made it possible to drop the $\Sigma(e_t x_{1t})$, ..., $\Sigma(e_t x_{k1})$ terms from the multiple linear regression formulation presented in (4.5-5).

6.3-3.   (1) $\ C_t = a_0 + a_1Y_t + a_2I_{t-1} + e_{1t}$

                        (2) $\ I_t = b_0 + b_1Y_t + e_{2t}$

                        (3) $\ Y_t = C_t + I_t$

A violation of the error term assumption that $E(e_t x_t) = 0$ occurs because an increase in e_{1t} and e_{2t} will cause C_t and I_t to increase. These increases in turn will increase Y_t via equation (3). But this increase in Y_t will increase Y_t in equations (1) and (2), thus leading to correlation between Y_t, e_{1t} and e_{2t}.

6.3-4.   Equation (1) is unidentified since there are no exogenous variables excluded from that equation. Equation (2) is exactly identified since the one excluded exogenous variable in equation (1) is equal to the one endogenous variable (Y_t) included as an explanatory equation in equation (2).

6.3-5.   For example, $S_t = b_0 + b_1P_t + b_2P_{t-1}$

6.3-6.   For example, $S_t = b_0 + b_1P_t + b_2P_{t-1} + b_3Y_t$

6.3-7.   The indirect least squares estimation approach or the TSLS estimation approach can be used to estimate the exactly identified demand equation as respecified in Exercise 6.3-5. Since unique values of the structural coefficients cannot be derived in an overidentified equation, only the TSLS estimation can be used in estimating the overidentified demand equation as specified in Exercise 6.3-6.

Computer Exercises:

6.3-8. $I_t = a_0 + a_1(Y_{t-1} - T_{t-1}) + e_t$

                         $C_t = C_t$

                         $G_t = G_t$

                         $Y_t = C_t + I_t + G_t$

```
>FETCH DSY IRE INR
>GENR ITO=IRE+INR
>SMPL 65.2 83.4
>LS ITO C DSY(-1)
```

```
SMPL  1965.2 - 1983.4
75 Observations
LS // Dependent Variable is ITO
=====================================================================
        VARIABLE    COEFFICIENT   STD. ERROR    T-STAT.    2-TAIL SIG.
=====================================================================
           C        1.9972291     6.0288831     0.3312768    0.741
        DSY(-1)     0.2217381     0.0047174    47.004325     0.000
=====================================================================
R-squared                0.968016    Mean of dependent var   255.6813
Adjusted R-squared       0.967578    S.D. of dependent var   129.2297
S.E. of regression      23.26921     Sum of squared resid    39526.31
Durbin-Watson stat       0.152408    F-statistic             2209.407
Log likelihood        -341.4417
=====================================================================
```

6.3-9.

> *>FETCH CUN DSY GEX IRE INR*
> *>GENR ITO=IRE+INR*
> *>SMPL 65.2 83,4*
> *>TSLS CUN C DSY @ C GEX ITO*

```
SMPL  1965.2 - 1983.4
75 Observations
TSLS // Dependent Variable is CUN
Instrument list: C GEX ITO
=====================================================================
        VARIABLE    COEFFICIENT   STD. ERROR     T-STAT.    2-TAIL SIG.
=====================================================================
           C       -17.622668     3.2307442    -5.4546776    0.000
          DSY        0.9230534     0.0024717   373.44982      0.000
=====================================================================
R-squared                0.999477    Mean of dependent var   1062.596
Adjusted R-squared       0.999470    S.D. of dependent var    541.2012
S.E. of regression      12.46270     Sum of squared resid    11338.28
Durbin-Watson stat       0.677801    F-statistic             139475.4
Log likelihood        -294.6123
=====================================================================
```

The ordinary least square estimated regression equation obtained in Computer Session 4.2-1 is

CUN = -16.625 + 0.922 DSY
   (-6.23)(376.88)

n = 76 from 1965.1 - 1983.4

The results of the TSLS estimate of the equation are extremely similar to those shown in the OLSQ estimate.

6.3-10.   >*FETCH CUN DSY GEX IRE INR*
            >*GENR ITO=IRE+INR*
            >*SMPL 65.3 83.4*
            >*TSLS CUN C DSY AR(1) @ C GEX ITO CUN(-1) DSY(-1)*

            SMPL 1965.3 - 1983.4
            74 Observations
            TSLS // Dependent Variable is CUN
            Instrument list: C GEX ITO CUN(-1) DSY(-1)
            Convergence achieved after 1 iterations
            ==

VARIABLE	COEFFICIENT	STD. ERROR	T-STAT.	2-TAIL SIG.
C	-19.241456	7.2824020	-2.6421854	0.010
DSY	0.9241962	0.0053109	174.02019	0.000
AR(1)	0.6572582	0.0891832	7.3697572	0.000

            ==
            R-squared   0.999699   Mean of dependent var   1071.222
            Adjusted R-squared   0.999691   S.D. of dependent var   539.6800
            S.E. of regression   9.487133   Sum of squared resid   6390.404
            Durbin-Watson stat   2.046879   F-statistic   118076.9
            Log likelihood   -269.9655
            ==

6.3-11.   >*FETCH GNP MNS GEX TFG*
            >*GENR BUD=TFG-GEX*
            >*SMPL 65.2 83.4*
            >*GENR CGNP=((((GNP-GNP(-1))/ABS(GNP(-1)))+1)^4-1)*100*
            >*GENR CMNS=((((MNS-MNS(-1))/ABS(MNS(-1)))+1)^4-1)*100*
            >*GENR CBUD((((BUD-BUD(-1))/ABS(BUD(-1)))+1)^4-1)*100*
            >*SMPL 66.1 83.4*
            >*TSLS CGNP C PDL(CMNS) PDL(CBUD) @ C CMNS(-1) CMNS(-2)*
            CMNS(-3) CBUD(-1) CBUD(-2) CBUD(-3) CGNP(-1) CGNP(-2)
            CGNP(-3)

            PDL Parameters for CMNS
            Number of lags? _3_
            Order of Polynomial? _2_
            Zero Constraints? _0_

            PDL Parameters for CGEX
            Number of lags? _3_
            Order of Polynomial? _2_
            Zero Constraints? _0_

141

```
PDL Parameters for CBUD
Number of lags? 3
Order of Polynomial? 2
Zero Constraints? 0

SMPL  1966.1 - 1983.4
72 Observations
TSLS // Dependent Variable is CGNP
Instrument list: C CMNS(-1) CMNS(-2) CMNS(-3) CBUD(-1) CBUD(-2) CBUD
(-3) CGNP(-1) CGNP(-2) CGNP(-3)
```

VARIABLE	COEFFICIENT	STD. ERROR	T-STAT.	2-TAIL SIG.
C	5.7847434	2.5366093	2.2805023	0.026
PDL1	-0.1897368	0.3580632	-0.5298974	0.598
PDL2	0.9082898	0.4820224	1.8843309	0.064
PDL3	-0.2954954	0.1304346	-2.2654687	0.027
PDL4	-4.237D-08	7.894D-08	-0.5367901	0.593
PDL5	3.421D-08	8.923D-08	0.3833767	0.703
PDL6	-8.515D-09	2.230D-08	-0.3818493	0.704

R-squared	0.116713	Mean of dependent var	9.190913
Adjusted R-squared	0.035179	S.D. of dependent var	4.596808
S.E. of regression	4.515228	Sum of squared resid	1325.173
Durbin-Watson stat	1.948228	F-statistic	1.431466
Log likelihood	-207.0183		

```
    Lag Distribution of CMNS      Lag   Coef     S.E.    T-Stat
===================================================================
|*            :                 |  0  -0.18974  0.35806 -0.52990
|             :               * |  1   0.42306  0.12098  3.49695
|             :              *|  2   0.44486  0.14706  3.02496
|      *      :                 |  3  -0.12433  0.15858 -0.78402
-------------------------------------------------------------------

         0                       Sum   0.55386  0.37697  1.46923
===================================================================
    Lag Distribution of CBUD      Lag   Coef     S.E.    T-Stat
===================================================================
|*                             :|  0  -4.2D-08  7.9D-08 -0.53679
|                   *          :|  1  -1.7D-08  2.2D-08 -0.74534
|                        *     :|  2  -8.0D-09  2.2D-08 -0.37094
|                   *          :|  3  -1.6D-08  2.3D-08 -0.72128
-------------------------------------------------------------------

                         0  Sum  -8.3D-08  9.6D-08 -0.86564
===================================================================
```